Preface

The title of this book almost was "Diamonds in the Dustpan," chosen to underscore the notion that sorting through even a collection of something so absolutely worthless as dust might produce the occasional gem.

That working title was quickly discarded on the basis of presumptuousness and because essentially this is a book about Pittsburgh, by my definition a sprawl of a soulful place that geographically encompasses the land bordered by the flatness of Ohio on the West, Altoona or so to the East, South to where they take offense at being called a "hoopie" and North to that point where the trees begin to outnumber the residents. In short, to wherever people answer "Pittsburgh" to the question "where you from?"

In the pages that follow, Pittsburgh, then, is seen less as a locale and more, much more, as a state of mind. No, that's too tony for Pittsburgh. An attitude. A way of looking at life and how it should properly be lived.

We are a little different hereabouts, I think. More inclined than most to emotion, to bending to the task, to a heartiness of spirit and a soul given to occasional fits of weeping. To holding fast to what has been and mistrusting change. To feeling more than thinking; to acting hastily more than inaction. In toto, to preferring whiskey and a beer chaser to any byproduct of grapes.

Can I offer evidence to support those contentions? Documentation? Nope, not a bit. Are they generalizations? Yes, to a certain degree. I simply know them the way historians say that Americans know their Constitution...in the bones.

Beyond this preface are the observations, musings and occasional rantings of one native to this place. Someone firmly snagged by middle age who, too, tends to cleave to what was and regard what is and what might be with some skepticism.

Outgrowing an incarnation as a sportswriter, I wrote roughly 1,500 general columns in the Pittsburgh Press, five per week, between early in 1983 and the summer of 1987. This collection was drawn from my first year or so of chasing after, but rarely catching, the essence of this place. Also a bit of presumptuousness on my part. As is the very idea of anthologies such as this one.

In truth, their only legitimate reason for existence is that they afford the interested reader the opportunity to return to the past and bring to it a perspective altered by the passage of time. Gathered and bound, they have the modest ambition of allowing leisurely reflection on what was and represent no more than a brief glimpse of a place and a time. After ▓▓▓▓▓▓▓▓▓▓▓▓▓▓▓▓▓▓▓▓▓ ▓
short—or on occasion, overblown—afterw▓▓▓▓▓▓▓▓▓▓▓▓▓▓▓ ▓
bring you up to speed on the subject; at oth▓

altered, I noted it.

There is no instructional manual for newspaper columnists; they vary much in the manner of the spectrum. From Mike Royko's arching wit and street wisdom to Dave Barry's outrageous humor to the various Washington pundits' heavy-handedness and invariable visions of doom. Local writers are not very different: Tom Hritz' last angry Everyman to Peter Leo's witty charm to Brian O'Neill's whimsy.

As you will shortly discover, I was a Rand McNally sort, searching the Pittsburgh map for what I perceived to be those people and stories that best reflected us and what we were all about at the moment. Sometimes *in extremis*, in the belief that we can find the sharpest focus at the hard edges of existence.

The reader of this work is asked for a certain indulgence. A number of these columns were written in first-person with this rationale: In what was happening in my life, you were likely to find the stuff of your own. And somehow be comforted, or at least have company in your misery or odd triumph. Some of the players, of course, have come and gone. For the sake of clarity, The Lady referred to is my ex-wife, whose attorney surely belongs in the Divorce Lawyers Hall of Fame and who, sadly enough, I have not seen in some years. The Bright-Eyed Girl is no less shiny these days, off in furious pursuit of her own life and now unencumbered in the search for that elusive prey, happiness. She remains what she has long been, one of the best friends anyone could hope to have. A professional in the world of words, she trussed up more than one dangling participle and retrieved many lost and forlorn gerunds in this book. The kids of whom I wrote, in spite of the handicap of my often over-reaching attempts at guidance, continue to thrive, one and all. References to The Blonde, to whom this is dedicated, will shortly become clear.

Some of the people about whom I wrote proved untraceable, beyond the reach of reasonable research. The girl who almost had a baby in the Allegheny County Jail, for example. Or the old man who lived in a drainage pipe. Others were located easily enough, like Downtown saloonkeeper and growling entrepreneur Steve Morris. A number have died, a truly courageous mother among them. I owe them all, and know that any failure in telling their stories was not in the least theirs.

Finally, the goal herein is simple enough: To have you discover in the people of these pages something of yourself and to come to a bit keener appreciation of a place more colorful, more passionate, more diverse, more robust and more indomitable than most.

Phil Musick
August 18, 1994
Pittsburgh, Pennsylvania

The Best of Phil Musick

Pittsburgh Places — Pittsburgh People

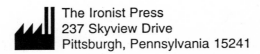

The Ironist Press
237 Skyview Drive
Pittsburgh, Pennsylvania 15241

Material in Pittsburgh Places, Pittsburgh People first appeared in
The Pittsburgh Press

Published in Pittsburgh by The Ironist Press, 237 Skyview Drive, Pittsburgh, Pennsylvania 15241

ISBN 0-964-1355-1-5

Cover photo courtesy of
James Lorenze
Superior Photo • 641 E. Brockway Avenure • Morgantown, WV • 26505

Cover and book design by
Daniel I. Morris
Visual Communication Associates • 4 Central Plaza • Waynesburg, PA 15370
(412) 852-2251

Manufactured in the United States of America

The First One For The
Blonde From Bailey Avenue

Loved you yesterday
Love you still
Always have
Always will

How does columnist like city? Let him count the ways

MASTER DAVID SANTA, a 9-year-old scholar at Hoover School in Mt. Lebanon, whose penmanship and lean prose style are admirable for any age, has written to pose an intriguing question:

"What do you like about Pittsburgh?"

His inquiry, part of an important class project called "Celebrate Pittsburgh," merits considerable interest from one who is native to this place and holds it in a certain affection.

What do I like about Pittsburgh?

Where to begin? With the people, whose passion is such that they have to speak with their hands as well as their mouths, presumably because they have so much to say that speech alone is found wanting? Where else do you suppose that Myron Cope would be a sex symbol?

Or with the neighborhoods, the ethnic roots of which are sunk so deeply as to resist even time? Where else can you play boccie and buy a pierogi in the same block?

Or with our institutions, just different enough that we have managed to foster a political Mafia peopled by the Irish, house a fine university largely in a single building, and place at the focal point of our commercial area a lovely park with a fountain?

I guess, David, that I like a thousand things about Pittsburgh. Which, at the outset, I would define not so much as a political subdivision, but a sprawling, hilly slash of geography roughly bounded by, say, the sad, hushed mills of the Beaver Valley to the west, the Laurel Mountains to the east, Butler to the north and the farms of Greene County to the south. And, of course, completely encircled by the only people in the world who regularly use the pronoun "yuns."

That seems broad enough to include anybody who identifies with Pittsburgh and not unnecessarily hurt anyone's feelings.

Mostly, I suspect, I like the people hereabouts.

Not the flawless sort of solid citizenry of which they brag on KDKA, those from good, old "Someplace Special" who eat a zillion Farkleberry Tarts for the sake of Children's Hospital; but the ones who bring to life around here a quicker pulse than I have discovered elsewhere. Nowhere that I've been are people so constrained to touch one another. Be it snatching a purse or in rough affection.

I am mindful about here of a silent exchange I witnessed one Downtown rush-hour evening a few months back between a crippled old man and an athletic young one. The young man took the old gentleman's elbow and guided him safely across a busy street. On the far sidewalk, the unsmiling old man nodded once, yanked his elbow free and resolutely tottered away, regathering his pride. The young man swore softly, then had to shake his head and grin.

Pittsburgh Places — Pittsburgh People

Pittsburgh folk, those two.

Thinking further on your question, David, it strikes me that what I like most about this place is its genuine disparity—I can imagine no other place with restaurants owned by six different people named Tambellini—and the elements in it that meet smoothly in concert.

The city at night from Mount Washington, red and yellow ribbons of light streaming out from the Point to the horizon, and the heartfelt belief that my claim on it is equal to that of any other. And the memories that magnificent view evokes of when I was a big-eyed kid and flames from the J&L mill on Second Avenue would leap a hundred feet into the night sky, and I thought this surely was the very hub of the universe.

The flames are gone now, along with other things that still trigger vague longings in me. The cool bar and hot music of the Hurricane, a jazz joint in the Hill. East Liberty, when it was a town all its own and not an awkward, jerry-built mall, full of junkies with glazed eyes. The North Hills, when stretches of woods flanked McKnight Road before the infestation of fast-food places.

Still, there are redeeming features around here too numerous to note. Flagstaff Hill in the purplish summer twilight, and the Strip teeming at 2 a.m. And I-79 where it cuts a swath through the rolling greenery of Washington County. The back roads of Fox Chapel, shaded by the limbs of 100-year-old oaks that guard the privacy of the rich. Shadyside, not the plastic facades of gaucherie on Walnut Street, but the neat brick homes with wrought-iron fences that march with real charm up Kentucky Avenue. The bubbling of Bloomfield, the quiet corridors of Carnegie Museum, the gothic spires on old-world homes that retrieve Mt. Lebanon from the tedium of suburbia. Awakening East Carson Street, old women in babushkas hurrying to the market in a babble of greeting.

I like the obscure spots; the ones I'm sure that I, alone, know. Turning down the steep cobblestone roller coaster of a street that connects Webster Avenue in the upper Hill with Bigelow Boulevard and, in one long, lurching drop, gives you quick peeks at Polish Hill, Lawrenceville and Garfield. The park up on Bailey Avenue on the back side of Mount Washington that lends the city a wholly different perspective than you can get from anyplace else.

I like the still places. The Point fountain on a 5-degree day when it's snowing so hard that only the lonely are there. Highland Park's reservoirs just after dawn. The town square in Ligonier late on a Sunday afternoon.

And, finally, I like the pace of life around here. Quick-step, for the most part. A friend of mine once said the iron-imperative here was taking care of business and I agree.

"Someplace Special" remains a transparent and clumsy attempt at seducing the loyalties of people who listen to the radio. Still, Pittsburgh is some place. And special.

I know it, this fine stew of a place, in my bones. The way Americans know the Constitution even if many cannot even number the Bill of Rights. The way the idle rich know sloth and the poor and desperate know work. In truth, I somewhat pity those who know it less well, or experience it only through their eyes and ears. Is there an adequate metaphor to define Pittsburgh? Probably not, or if there is, it's beyond my reach. The only one that comes to mind is a struck tuning fork...vibrating endlessly. What we were in this place, largely we are no more. Steel has departed, along with it the tens of thousands of attendant jobs. Now we are in thriving transition; becoming something new and different. Remaking ourselves in a single generation. Yet we remain what generations of us were, a people and a place more vital than most. Or it appears that way to the incurably romantic among us.

Plucky Cambodians wake up the American dream

IF CYNICISM HAS stolen our vision of it, rest assured the old and out-of-vogue American Dream is alive and well, and can be viewed daily in the Eastern suburbs.

Currently, the very best of it is in possession of the five Srun kids, who have survived the hardest of life's knocks and proven no more resolute than the tide.

Not long ago residents of a Cambodian jungle clearing, they have been all but swallowed whole by the new culture and can now be seen in Pirate caps, Disney sweat shirts and eye shadow, saved from the clutches of the popular blathering of "y'know" only by the mailed fist of their chief adviser.

This, then, is by way of announcing a very special occasion. Were it possible, the newspaper you are holding would shoot fireworks against the ceiling.

It is precisely two years to the day that the Sruns—four boys, one girl, one courageous mother—migrated from Cambodia, arriving at Greater Pitt in a spate of botched arrangements, empty bellies, weary eyes and, somewhat biblically, led down the jetway by a small child.

He would be Samnoun (Som-NEW-un) Srun, a smallish 8 at the time, his assertiveness later traced to sleeping through dinner on the airplane. Behind him—pale, stick-thin, airsick and timid—trailed his older siblings, thrown up on freedom's shores by tragic circumstance and the good offices of the Catholic Church.

Somewhere there is a picture of them taken in a Thai refugee camp. Heads shaved too slick for even head lice. Numbers strung convict-fashion across their chests. Hollow eyes. Today, those eyes usually shine, particularly in the presence of ice cream, new jeans, a flourishing vegetable garden and textbooks. Each of which is regularly ravished.

The Sruns were victims of a Cambodian madman named Pol Pot, who claimed 1 million lives in a holocaust the world continues to ignore, perhaps because it tripped on the heels of another. Understand, for what was lost, they grieve silently.

The details would dribble out late at night, softly, as they puzzled over their homework or thumbed a Cambodian-English dictionary to shreds. Father executed in the front yard by the Communists for the crime of having a fourth-grade education. Hiding weeks on end in mountain caves. A baby brother who starved to death. Samnoun, too weak to walk, carried to Thailand on his older brothers' backs. Two years behind barbed wire in a camp. Misery enough in just months for a lifetime. "It was hard," they say now.

And it's receding history. In the succeeding two years, they have managed to impart the lessons of gentleness, kindness, patience and warmth to some of the natives and thrive no more vigorously than crabgrass. All the while sponging up knowledge on any number of subjects, ranging from American history to algebra to whether God takes a shower.

Currently, they are mining the new world in the manner of the original settlers, piling up one victory after another while rubbing the callouses from the spirit of at least one Occidental.

For example, Samnang (Som-NANG), 14, whose smile is cheery enough to throw long shadows, has recently wrestled from the jungle of English idioms in her science text a basic understanding of the theory of convection. No mean accomplishment in the eyes of someone whose tongue has yet to cope with the Cambodian phrase for hello.

"Hot air rises...cool air comes in underneath...it rains!" She also washes a mean dish and is the only local teenager known to have suffered the ravages of adolescence gracefully. From her: Faith in the future.

For her four brothers, there have been similar triumphs, and few casts of characters have ever merited further description.

Sophea (So-PAY-uh), 16 and more of a man than most since he was 10, sacrificed his childhood to holding his family together through true horror and then survived another, touring ninth grade with a 3.4 QPA. Which is not bad for a kid who spoke no English 24 months ago and is still trying to understand all the fuss over George Washington throwing a silver dollar across the Rappahannock. He presently exhibits an increasingly healthy attitude toward Playboy magazine. From him: The example of strength.

Phanaa (Puh-NAW), 14, the sunniest, hardest-working kid alive, is continuously involved in saving a handyman of his acquaintance from himself. As was said of the great and good copy editor, "He is the salt of the earth and a joy forever." From him: A constancy of the heart.

Then, there is Phannak (Puh-NOCK), 12, who is rawboned, a tight end in the making who has put aside the temperament of his people for the aggressiveness and inquisitiveness of a young grizzly. When the grin falls from his face, his temperature is taken. From him: Balm for the soul.

Last, but...Samnoun, not long ago too sickly to walk to freedom, but currently the world champion of dinner and a leading contender in the breakfast and lunch divisions. One of the great lap-climbers of the modern era. From him: The gift of love.

There you have them, all-pro in the kid league. Fresh, new Americans and sterling evidence that, for all of our frailties and misplaced ideals and refugee quotas, this is still the best place for the huddled masses.

In October of 1981, my family grew by six...the Sruns. The details are somewhat complicated; suffice it to say that I became their sponsor; that they lived with my ex-wife and I for a year-and-a-half; that the kids do me the honor of calling me "Father" since I have pinch-hit for their Dad, and that I learned most of the important lessons of this life from them.

Like many who came to this country before them, they bent their backs to whatever the task, and thrived. In all ways.

An Update seems in order.

The family owns and operates two Chinese restaurants, one in New Castle, the other in Youngstown. Incidentially, the food is superb. Sophea manages the Youngstown location, his mother, Nay, and her husband, Tony, run the New Castle restaurant. An excellent chef, Phanna moves between the two as necessary. Samnang is the mother of three daughters, including twins. Phannak is in the United States Air Force and he and his wife, Sopaul, have a little girl. Samnoun--Sam—recently graduated from Neshannock High School and is headed off to college.

The years have not changed them at all. Not in the ways that count. I am not nearly accomplished enough as a writer to explain what it has meant to have them in my life. Joy is only a part of it.

Late October's chill rekindles a young man's regret

THE OLD MAN always brought a rich disdain to emergent autumn.

The wind would kick up, stripping the leaves from the maples and riding a chill into his vulnerable bones, and he would get crustier than usual and curse whatever poet came to mind. Robert Frost, usually.

I always bore some of the brunt of his disappointment in the approach of winter. Sometime in a dying October, it was my habit to sneak off to the Sugar Valley for a final inning with the sleepy trout on that stretch of Fishing Creek that passes through the tiny village of Loganton up in Clinton County. Arriving, I could usually hear him grousing 100 yards down the lane.

My grandmother would kiss me welcome and give me a look that said The Old Man's rheumatism was acting up and to beware his flinty temper. Truth was, he thought the Lord had blown it, locating Heaven anywhere but that lovely little valley, and when in late October he had to leave it, it grated mightily.

"No place else like this, boy," he would purr of a summer evening, when the fading sunlight had turned the distant ridges dusky rose and a little sour mash had worn down his bite.

He was never mellow; not even into his 87th year, which is when he fetched a young doctor an ungodly whack across the shins with his cane that rang like struck steel. But in that valley, if the copperheads knew to keep their distance, he was bearable.

Autumn, he held, was a time of death. Never mind that poetic nonsense. He'd been a newspaperman for almost seven decades by then and trenchant phrases had not been strangers, but he never trusted that fall would make way for fresh beginnings.

"The hell with tomorrow," he would grouch. "That's for you, boy."

The leaves would pile eye-high on the spring house before he began readying to leave "because it's getting too cold up here for your grandmother." She would turn her head and smile at that, because to laugh in the Old Man's face was to be turned to stone by his eyes.

Closing up the Hermitage, so named in honor of Andrew Jackson, was never a small task. That's what he called the place, maybe 30 acres of trees and farmland that peered majestically down on the valley floor from a perch halfway up Bald Eagle Mountain. He was a Jacksonian Democrat the way the Pope is a Catholic and by the time he was 70, he could chuckle that "maybe that's what I am now, an old hermit."

A last weekend of fishing he would tolerate, but between dawn and dusk, there were always closing up tasks. Some caulking. Replacing fence latches. Shoring up the stone wall along the lane. Spreading a fresh load of shale on it. Filling a slew of bird feeders.

Some particularly fine maple leaves were to be collected and pressed in the family Bible. He was dead before I knew they were not my grandmother's collection but his.

The Old Man would've scoffed if it had been suggested he was an incurable romantic about the Hermitage—but he never left the valley of an autumn before cramming a battered felt down over the gray stripe that circumnavigated his pink scalp and spending a whole day "checking the place out."

Likely as not, the skies drifting in from Nittany Valley and hovering over its tiny neighbor would be leaden; purple clouds, swollen with moisture, spitting a cold drizzle. Only Republicans and chilblains could make him grouchier.

"Boy and I are going out to look around," he would announce to my grandmother, as though she had ever once disputed him on a minor point, or I always suspected, yielded on a major one. And we would go, tromping crosscountry through the rotting sheaves so he could breach the small stone wall that marked his land at a juncture that needed minor repairs.

I would affect them; he would, as was his wont, closely study some subject at hand and broaden my education. One time it would be maples, limbs flowing russet and deep gold. "Pretty tree...syrup is overrated."

Another time, stones. "Always clean the moss off, dig a good trough before you lay them; stop cows better than barbed wire." Another time, the season itself. "The Lord makes it for a purpose, I suppose."

He would rub the cold from his arms, thin and pale and harder than stone, and grouse about the coming winter. Still, the last look was ritual and, if I'd been just a little older and more sure of myself, he would've gotten it the year he died.

That he did not, I blamed myself for into my 40s. A busted hip that wouldn't mend had him flat when old age finally wore him away at 87. In the hospital one day near the end, he said, "Boy, I'd like to see the place once more," and not another word. I mumbled something reassuring.

My Dad, my uncles and the doctors all said the trip might kill him, so he never made it and, in weeks, I was overseas. He died a month or so later. My regret that I'd let him down in his autumn hung on for years.

The regret, all these years later, lingers. The time you should have stood up, intractable, and did not. We must all have such moments. The valley, of course, remains...in Spring and early Autumn lush and without equal among such treasured places. The Amish have come in numbers and it fairly hums with their industriousness and resolve to hold life simply. I return rarely; one of my relatives owns the Hermitage. She appreciated neither the rare beauty nor the Old Man's mighty soul. I remember both. He set the standard for grandfathers, the Old Man did.

Bo's ninth life ended as the first began—with dignity

HE WASN'T EXACTLY a Prince of a cat. An Earl, maybe. No, he was a Baron. Large. Imperious. A rangy, Seal-point of a Siamese. Black and tan, with the dignity and bearing of a 16th century Pope.

He has gone now to whatever place the Lord reserves for felines that live richly, die well, and leave a fitting example of how to be a cat for whatever kittens have been fortunate enough to cross their paths. He was 15 and, sadly, it was time.

His name was Bo, the affectionate diminutive of B.O., the moniker he acquired as a young fellow slow to learn the breed's innate good grooming habits. Meticulous beyond kittenhood, he became Bo. Strangers were told it was short for Beauregard, and his regal bearing could easily have been mistaken for Southern courtliness.

The Lady of the house was present at his birth to Tinkerbell, a fine old matron, and he was mostly a one-woman cat right there to the end. By the time we got acquainted, both of us were approaching middle age at flank speed and firmly set in our ways.

For my part, having loved cats from boyhood, I was adamant that he would shortly reciprocate, offering me both allegiance and devotion.

"A sure pop," I told his mistress. "He'll be sitting on my lap in a matter of days."

It required the better part of five years to turn that neat trick; Bo was no easy seduction. For him, there was the lady; Kim, who'd shared youth with him, and Kyle, whose rough affection he tolerated with the patience of a saint until the years gentled it. There was no one else.

"Give him some time," was the lady's counsel.

Lord knows, it took a full measure. I have very few regulations for the animals in my life, but an unyielding one is that they do not tarry on the shadowy stairs from the kitchen to the basement. That, I do not allow, having once damn near somersaulted down a whole flight of steps over the heaving form of a beagle, who nipped me in the calf as I sailed past for disturbing him.

Bo viewed the stairs as a fine place to doze. Not as comfortable as the laundry basket, you understand, but suitable.

For years, our positions remained chiseled in stone. He would slumber on the steps; on watch while using them, I would nudge him with a toe. Or, especially irritated, a brisk instep. His ears would ride down on his head as he sauntered downstairs, his clear contempt marking me for the bully that I was.

Otherwise, our relationship grew as wine ages—slowly, but with unmistakable change. In time, I was permitted to scratch his chin, which he enjoyed no more than a sea bass, and he would speak to me.

Yeah, Bowie could talk. Low, mournful howls, rich with meaning, whether seeking his supper, or noting that the litter box was ripening, or to just tell you his chin felt terrific. Agitated, though, his ears would flatten, his eyes narrowing in indictment, and the howls would grow deeper and quicker.

"He's disgusted," the lady would always laugh.

As he was the night he won a war of wills with Tim Menees, a friend and the Post-Gazette cartoonist. Menees plays what is quite possibly the most raucous honkytonk piano in the world and one night at our place, he was never more frenzied.

The trouble was that he was sitting on the bench Bo habitually reserved for those Sunday afternoons when he curled up beside his mistress as she knocked the rust from her piano skills.

While Tim was banging out, "Great Balls of Fire," Bo joined him on the bench, ears flat. Menees brooks absolutely no interference in celebrating his beloved 50s rock and roll. The stalemate—poundingly loud on Tim's part, silent conviction on Bo's—lasted a full half-hour. Menees retreated.

No one ever demonstrated more decorum under fire than Bo did that night and his dignity was no less intact when kidney failure struck him late last week.

He found a fat piece of carpeting next to the basement wash tub, eased down upon it, tucked his forepaws under his chest like the sphinx he was and gracefully awaited his fate.

The collie would amble over from time to time, his instincts telling him something was amiss. Bo would fix him with a baleful stare and he'd retreat and Bo would quietly wait some more.

Hurting the last few days, he was stoic, yielding only a few howls when forced to move. The vet did what he could; the lady, too. Finally it was clear that a cat who'd been noble in life deserved a peaceful end to it.

Kyle, who seemed to go through puberty with Bo resignedly strung around his neck, went down to the basement for a while Saturday morning. Later that afternoon, while the man of the house was in an airplane, he and the lady took Bo to the vet for the last time.

"Bowie didn't fuss a bit," the lady said rather proudly when the tears stopped.

No, he wouldn't have.

Cat people—we seem to instantly recognize one another as though our foreheads were marked like Hawthorne's Hester Prynne—often encounter a Bowie. Cats with a regal indifference; a challenge to our unassailable belief that no feline is immune to our charm. We like or love them no less than the others, just differently. As with old lovers, the memories of them recede slowly. The lady and I took separate paths not long after Bo fled this vale of tears; doubtless she remembers, as I do, an old cat with more dignity than even a Baron.

His struggle to care for bedridden wife a lonely one

THERE IS an old gag.

A guy goes into a confessional and tells a priest, "I'm having an affair with a beautiful married woman."

The priest directs penance.

"I don't know the words to say the Hail Marys, I'm not Catholic," the guy explains.

"Then why are you here?" asks the priest.

"I'm so excited, I had to tell somebody."

Fred is like the guy in the story. He has to tell somebody.

Fred is 69 years old; warm, out-going, articulate even when he's deep in the sauce. The work ethic caught him early. You hustle, you save, you take care of your own...there comes a day when your feet go up and someone slips a cold gin-and-tonic in your fist and a rocking chair under your back pockets.

One day, those old beliefs withered and blew away. He took a wife with a cold to a doctor and got back a vegetable. He looked around for help, and was told to come back after he'd used up his last dime.

"No one can help me or her...except Jesus Christ," he was saying yesterday afternoon, booze having worn the edges of every word smooth. "Not until I spend my last dollar."

But I got to tell someone." He laughs. "A psychologist, it costs me $200 and I got worse bills."

Fred's wife has multiple sclerosis. She's paralyzed.

"The only thing that moves are her eyes," he says flatly. Often there is pity for her in his voice; occasionally love. Mostly he talks about her as though she were driftwood.

They had been separated for a long time, grew in different directions. But he's 69, from the old school.

"I'm old-fashioned," he says. "You pay your freight, cradle to grave."

The freight is oppressive. His wife went to a doctor for a bad cold. She got lumbar pneumonia. Then came the MS. One day they brought her home with a tube in her stomach and another in her throat.

Fred has cared for her since. Once, he loved her; now she's an obligation.

"I got a private hospital in my house," Fred says. "She came home, there was so much machinery on her, it blew out every fuse in the house."

He coughs and apologizes. Don't misunderstand, he says. Bitching is futile, for suckers. He learned that a long time ago. He just wonders why there isn't some way he can get a little help.

"You're hearing me at a bad time," he says. "I drink to keep from blowing my head off. Luckily, I got two daughters. She needs constant care, to feed her, drain her lungs, move her. They work 12-hour shifts.

"I tried to hire nurses. They want $81; that's for an eight-hour shift."

The money is going. Fred isn't flat-broke, he laughs, but it's just a matter of time. His wife has to be maintained in a totally germ-free environment, handled with sterile equipment.

"One germ, she could go," he says. You can hear his voice searching for that germ.

She is fed intravenously. It requires two-and-a-half cases of formula per week; at $71.50 a case.

He wrote a letter to the company that makes the formula. Heart transplant Barney Clark had caught the nation's fancy about then. Maybe there was a little charity to be had.

"They wrote back and told me there were bleeding for me," he says with rich disgust. "Told me who had the local franchise for the stuff. And sent me a free case.

"I need help."

Fred won't get it. Not from the government. "I owned a couple properties, a little business. Till I go broke, no one can help." Not from the MS Society: "They say they don't have much money." Not from any private source: "You see her now, a beautiful woman she once was, you'd throw your bank account on her bed."

There's no end to this story. For now, Fred estimates it costs $60,000 a year to keep his wife alive: "I have to go, or she does, before there will be any help.

"I should be in Florida somewhere with my feet up."

In this place, more than most, we prize indomitability. Around here, the iron imperative is: Get it done. Bitch if you have to, but do it. So Fred did it. And one afternoon when the doing became damn near intolerable, he called a guy to muse for a bit about the vagaries of this life and how the gods were not always generous. No last name, he said. It didn't matter. Said he thought there were probably a lot of people in worse shape than he was. Didn't want pity, or even empathy. Said he might call back one day with an update; to tell me how it all worked out. He never did. Maybe he is sitting somewhere with his feet up, frosty gin-and-tonic in his fist. Pretty to think so.

Trial hurts mother almost as much as daughter's rape

THE PLAYHOUSE was almost dark, a couple of candles throwing flickering shadows on the walls as the three teen-age boys tried to whisper up their nerve.

Terry was afraid. The nearby house where her playmate lived was dark. She knew her mother didn't know where she was and would be worried. But Terry was tired of always having to play with the little kids; of being bigger and slower to understand games and being treated differently. And of the older kids not liking her.

"You want a boyfriend, don't you?" the boys asked. Other girls her age had boyfriends. They held hands. Laughed together. Had fun. Acted sort of like her Mom and Dad. Terry nodded.

"That's what girls do with their boyfriends," the boys insisted.

Did they? Really? Terry was confused.

"Nothing bad will happen to you," the boys assured, fumbling with her clothes.

Terry is 12, and so pretty people often comment on it, and retarded. And a boyfriend would be nice.

When she felt the pain and got so scared she couldn't move, it was too late. Rape?

The doctor who examined Terry at Children's Hospital didn't have a doubt. "Multiple rape." The cops and a counselor from Pittsburgh Action Against Rape agreed.

A judge didn't.

"As horrifying to us as the rape was the way it was handled," Terry's mother was saying yesterday. "The charges were suddenly dismissed. I left the courtroom in shock."

Terry left it happy enough with herself. The judge, her mother remembers, had scolded the boys. "I'm convinced something very bad happened in that playhouse!"

By then, Terry realized something very bad had happened. But the judge called her "a very beautiful girl" and seemed nice when he was telling her not to go into playhouses with boys. And she was glad to be away from the large, formal room and the boys sitting near her and everyone acting very serious. Mostly, she was glad the questions were over.

"The issue was consent," Terry's mother says. "She's mildly-retarded emotionally. Slow. Not a normal 12-year-old. She couldn't give her consent. She doesn't understand. She couldn't imagine the seriousness or the consequences."

The attorney representing the three boys—two 13-year-olds, one 14—asked Terry what year she was born. She couldn't remember. Could she tell time? She couldn't. Make change? No. But Terry did realize one thing. When she said no, the questions went faster.

"Did you scream, Terry?"

"No."

"Did they tie you up?"

"No."

"Did they lock you up?"

"No."

And the damning question. She had, on her own, returned to the playhouse while the boys were still there. Maybe to find a boyfriend.

"Did you go back, Terry?"

"Yes."

Terry's mother understood what was happening; realized her daughter was the poorest possible witness.

"She used that...'No,' or 'I don't know'...as a way out of her embarrassment," Terry's mother says.

Much of the anger she felt toward the boys has worn away with time—leaving in its wake frustration and a bitterness that the system somehow did not work.

What does she want? Revenge? Retribution? Some measure of flesh to pay for a 12-year-old confused girl's pain and fear and embarrassment?

"Something," she sighs. "There was no probation. No order to them to stay away from her. That was the outcome. Nothing."

Not quite. There is Terry, worried that her Mom and the police and everyone else in the neighborhood won't believe her when she says it wasn't her fault. There is Terry thinking maybe she did something bad. That maybe she is bad.

There is that.

And, of course, there is the possibility that one day there may be another Terry in her neighborhood. As Terry's mother says, "Those boys learned something...they learned they could get away with rape."

Terry doesn't understand that. She knows that her mother won't let her go very far from the house now. That there are only the little kids to play with. That she must forget about a boyfriend. But the trial is a vague memory now, except for the last few minutes. She is proud of the way it ended. And she says often:

"I did good, didn't I? Everyone said I did!"

The judge is still around, as big a fool as he was that day. There were reasons why he couldn't be identified then; there are reasons now. Terry's last name couldn't be used for obvious reasons. Her mother is still angry. Long ago, the incident retreated from Terry's memory; perhaps the feelings, too, have gone. The three boys are adults. Maybe the ancient thinker was right and what goes around, comes around. There are, of course, many Terrys. This one still doesn't have a boyfriend.

Late paying bill, she finds gas company isn't equitable

EQUITABLE GAS CO.'s logotype is a benign little flame in a circle.

Peggy Schwilm of McCandless, who has been doing business with the utility for longer than she cares to remember, figures the logotype should be changed: To a smoking pistol on a rampant field of black masks and vertical steel bars.

Peggy Schwilm is angry. Like the mad broadcaster in the movie "Network." She got a letter from Equitable the other day, requiring her to post a $200 bond. Her crime? She'd been late with the gas bill. Four kids, a husband who works as a steamfitter and a troubled economy will bring about such tardiness.

Used to be, paying a utility bill late was commonplace. After you missed the date a half-dozen times, you got a gentle reminder from the utility which cherished your business.

"You've been late with the payment, Miz Schwilm," an apologetic telephone voice would say. "Maybe your husband's out of work? Lot of medical bills? You've been overdoing it on the numbers, perhaps? Can we work something out?"

Nowadays, empathy comes from a computer. It belches a printout: Peggy Schwilm has blown it on the bill four times the last 12 months. Bring the death squad back from El Salvador.

Equitable explains it has a new policy. The hammer is something called a "deposit program." This is a nice euphemism, Peggy Schwilm thinks, for grand larceny. She had not heard of this new policy, she explains. "Underhanded" and "sneaking" are words that come to her.

Equitable will, the letter explains, hold Peggy Schwilm's 200 bucks for the remainder of 1984. It will even pay 11 percent interest on the money. Unless the payments are late. Then, Equitable will put the $200 to another use.

There are circles in which this procedure is known as a form of loan sharking and the guys who come around to collect have a lot of hair on their hands. Equitable calls it "a deposit program." Peggy Schwilm thinks of it along the lines of clipping pennies from the eyes of the newly fallen.

"Highway robbery," she says. "Our bills are so extremely high, it's impossible to always get the money there on time. The last bill was $223, the one before that $168. But..."

It is the "but" that is interesting and at the crux of Peggy Schwilm's ill feeling toward Equitable. She has paid her gas bills, without stiffing the company even once, for 40 years. She thinks that she ought to have a little credibility with the gas company. Ah, sweet naivete.

When the gas company explains that nature has done it dirty and a line is busted, and so she won't be able to use her stove for a day or so, Peggy Schwilm understands. Who is she to question the Almighty? A gas line has broken. It happens. She'll cook on a hot plate. She'll pay her bill.

"Sure, we've been late a few times," she says, "but they have always been paid. Always. Equitable Gas never lost a dime dealing with us."

Her fealty being ignored is what puts the fire in Peggy Schwilm's words. Forty years is a lot of gas bills.

But Equitable understands.

"If customers have a problem, they should call us and we can work out a special payment schedule," says a man from Equitable.

"For five hours, I tried calling," Peggy Schwilm says. "I was on hold 45 minutes at a time. I called another number and asked for a customer representative, someone in charge. I was told: 'Absolutely not.'

"Finally, I managed to get another number and a woman there told me, 'I'm going crazy listening to screaming and crying customers, people who don't have the money to pay.'"

"We know that's a big problem," the man from Equitable says, "but we're working on it."

"You would think that after 40 years, they'd be a little understanding," Peggy Schwilm says.

"I can see why she'd feel that way," the man from Equitable says. "It goes back to the computer thing. The past doesn't matter, unfortunately. We're working on it."

Candor fairly explodes from his breast. "Basically, we're trying to get them to pay," he allows.

But Peggy Schwilm should take heart. Equitable is trying to find a method of giving a break to customers who've been reliable and honorable for 40 years. That problem will be rectified.

As soon as Equitable can locate a computer with a heart.

Alas, nobody has managed to locate a computer with either heart or soul, Equitable Gas included. As has been noted, the more things change, the more they stay the same. Peggy Schwilm got her gas bill paid; your hair still grows an inch while on hold for a utility company representative; for most of us, debt continues to outrun income; businesses remain convinced that public relations campaigns can offset their lack of service or compassion, and we keep truckin'. Occasionally, a Peggy Schwilm has had enough and some soulless corporate entity gets a small shiner. Life goes on, usually to the accompaniment of a recorded message telling us, "We're sorry, but all our customer representatives are busy...please hold...your call will be answered in the order it was received." Nobody, ever, says in a human voice, "Gee, we've done business with you for 40 years...we'll trust you." A pity, that.

Zemprelli pulls partner through drunk-driving loophole

IT IS WONDERFULLY COMFORTING to know that we have, right here in Western Pennsylvania, one of the great thinkers of our time. Clearly the possessor of what the Irish poet Donovan must've had in mind when he beseeched, "More brain, O' Lord, more brain." A man whose wisdom would've sent Solomon scurrying away, in red-faced awe.

This giant, of course, is state Sen. Edward Zemprelli, D-Clairton, and clearly a man intellectually gifted enough to consider great ethical questions and dispatch them with the ease with which the rest of us sneeze.

Take a situation involving ponderous legal machinery on one hand and on the other, something as basic as a man driving an automobile when tests indicate he would've been seriously pressed to grab his hindquarters with either hand. For Zemprelli, the resolution was a snap.

Edward Zemprelli, the Senate minority leader, is on record as an advocate of stiffer drunken-driving laws. He is also a strict interpreter of the letter of the law. That these elements clanged against one another thunderously in a recent case in which he was involved, seems not to have concerned him a twit.

It was Zemprelli's ability to separate the letter of the law from the spirit of the law that enabled his legal partner, David C. Clipper, to beat a drunken-driving charge Friday in Common Pleas court on a technicality so slim as not to impair the passage of light from a 25-watt bulb. That someone's conscience was twisted into a granny knot by what transpired and the charges against Clipper were reinstated today doesn't seem to be particularly pertinent.

It went down this way: Clipper was arrested in Whitehall in June and a Breathalyzer test revealed he had a blood-alcohol level of 0.169. In this state, a reading of .10 presumes a driver is smacked-up enough to be a prime candidate to either wind up with a tag on his big toe, or to cause that form of final identification to be applied to one or more innocents.

Enter the district attorney's office with a written complaint against Clipper, which was presumably drawn up by a first-year pre-law student with myopia. The complaint fatally failed to state to what degree Clipper was zonked.

Edward Zemprelli managed to pull his partner through that crack in due process and clear of Common Pleas Court Administrative Judge Robert Dauer's courtroom, to say nothing of the slammer.

"It's not a crime to operate a car under the influence," Dauer explained to the Post-Gazette. "The complaint must say to what degree that renders him incapable."

Various explanations were given as to precisely how Clipper temporarily escaped the mills of justice, all of which smacked of low comedy. One assistant DA said the defective complaint had been orally amended at a preliminary hearing. Clipper's other attorney—there are three partners in the firm—was unable to recall any such oral amendment. Chris Copetas, the first assistant district attorney, simply said his office had "mangled" the case, which in light of the result seems unduly generous. You are left to form your own conclusions in the matter.

Edward Zemprelli—protector of a citizen's right to walk or operate a vehicle in this Commonwealth without having to dodge cars driven by people whose eyes won't focus—was easily able to view the matter from all angles and still not see an ethical consideration.

"Why would I feel pangs of conscience on matters of the law?" he inquired of a reporter, whose subsequent control of her facial muscles must go down in physiological annals as a masterstroke comparable to the invention of the saddle block. "I call the decision justice—the system requires that a person must be charged with a crime and he (Clipper) wasn't."

Why would Edward Zemprelli feel pangs of conscience? Let us count the ways.

There might be one small pang for the injustice of a situation in which a guy almost slides through a loophole owing to someone's simple oversight, while hundreds of the less well-connected spend some period of their remorse being reminded of their misdeeds by the presence of steel bars. And another pang for sponsoring legislation one day and then cutting technically legal escape hatches in it the next. And another for putting your thumb against your nose and pointing four fingers at your constituents' overwhelming sentiments.

Death, taxes and politicians beyond the reach of law or simple ethics. Two Speakers of the United States House of Representatives, enough Congressmen to crew the Queen Elizabeth, and any number of sleazy state legislators have left public life in disgrace since this column took to task a politician who twisted law to his own purpose. But, then, a wise man once observed that people generally get the sort of government they deserve. Ed Zemprelli has gone to his reward; presumably, the partner involved has managed not to injure or kill anyone while in alcohol's grasp. Meanwhile, too often, we continue to choose unwisely those who govern us. Ollie North comes to mind here.

Sidewalk jazzman beats blues with cool street horn

SOMETIMES, he hunches his shoulders and blows a smoky riff of raunchy blues straight down onto the few wrinkled singles and loose change in the bottom of his open trumpet case.

Sometimes, he turns the horn upward, rises on his toes and sails long C-notes from a '40s ballad, as pure as a nun, up Fifth Avenue toward Smithfield, freezing pedestrians in mid-stride.

Always, he gives the customers their money's worth.

Oh, in the low registers, he occasionally struggles a bit, reaching for a few bars of a particularly funky bit of jazz. But on high, when he sucks up his diaphragm and girds his courage, you can hear young Ray Anthony. Or maybe Miles Davis in the early '60s, when they came to the Cotton Club in Harlem in waves to hear him blow "Bitches' Brew" piercingly enough to knock the plaster off the walls.

"I thought it was a way to get experience playing different kinds of music," Roger Woods is explaining just before a kid, 9 or 10, wearing a Pitt football cap and a Super Steelers jacket, edges close enough to drop a few coins into the case.

"Keeps food on the table," Woods says, easing his horn from the pavement and thanking the kid with a tight smile and a few soft bars of an old '30s tune, "Now's The Time."

The kid stands no more than three feet away, looking dead into the bell of the trumpet, unblinking. A young aficionado. A middle-aged woman in a $200 red raincoat stops, turns back, and almost gets run over by the man behind her.

Roger Woods is 41 years old; learned the horn a long, long time ago in a reform school. "Picked it up on my own," he says. And refined it some in the years when a fine lady named Birdie Dunlap brought some heavyweight horn players into the Hurricane up on the Hill.

Woods has the build and look of one of those aging, compact lightweights of 30 years ago that smart fighters side-stepped on their way to the top. Street-wise, steady eyes, tight leather jacket, a Greek fisherman's cap pulled low, all suggest he's done a lot of things for a living.

Mostly, he cooked. For a while, in a place called Boykin's in Homestead, where the barbecued ribs belonged in the pork hall of fame. But Boykin's closed, and one day Roger Woods took his horn Downtown, put the open case on the ground and started making his music.

"It was scary," he admits. "The fear of rejection. I struggled with it."

It's not easy, standing on Downtown sidewalks, putting what you do better than anything else out there on display for people in a hurry to stomp on with a dirty look, a snicker.

He picks up the horn again and nurses from it the forlorn wail of a Bunny

Berrigan tune. He likes it all. "If I said I didn't like pops, I'd be lying," he shrugs. "But I like jazz. I love the easy-listening stuff...the beautiful music."

A guy in a pearl-gray fedora and electric blue pimp-suit ambles over, his eyes rolling up in his head. He is higher than PPG Place.

"Bro, that's good!" he mumbles the words around in his mouth. He wants a hand slap; Woods gives him a quick, tentative handshake. The junkie is indignant. "Move it," Woods says very softly. The junkie drifts.

"There are a few weirdos, I just tell them to move along," he says. "Some shopkeepers complained when I first started. Called the cops."

That was a year ago. Roger Woods is a Downtown fixture now. Some days on Fifth in front of the Lerner Shop just off Wood, others along Liberty Avenue. Just playing his horn, the open case yawing at his feet, encouraging the grateful.

"I was never that good of a cook," he says. "I'd rather do something that I'm reasonably good at."

Roger Woods is good. Not great. Occasionally uneven after nights like Thursday. "Drank too much, not good for the diaphragm," he says.

Still, solid good. In his street horn, you can hear some of the old legends. Anthony's clarity, out there hanging 10 at the edge of control, but forever steady. Shorty Rogers' style. Art Farmer's soul. Miles, when he'd air out one note so that it would carry a mile and turn people to stone. Bits and pieces of greatness.

"They love it," he says quietly of his music, not bragging, just at one with those customers who love a good horn. "Especially when you play their favorites."

Woods plays them all. Jazz, pop, what you hear on WSHH. Somewhere between 200 and 300 tunes from memory. A mixed bag for "a mixed environment. I like to experiment."

On Christmas day, he came Downtown from his place on the Hill and blew a little life into the empty stone canyons. "Carols," he remembers. "I had a great time."

He's around even on the bitterest days. "When I get into the music," he says, "I forget about being cold."

On this fine afternoon, he and the horn are warm. A guy tosses a handful of change in the case and says so-long. Roger Woods says "Thanks" and picks up the horn.

A block away, you can still hear the sweet agony of Blue Moon.

He's still there, after all these years. In truth, the horn wasn't as good as I described it, but the commitment to playing it was even better. One Christmas afternoon a few years ago, I didn't see him, but I could hear his horn through the car window. Downtown, empty, cavernous. The day gray and mean, a stiletto wind blowing off the rivers and into the ribs. One note...clear and crisp and silvery, running

21

through the cold stillness until you knew it would disintegrate into a million tiny fragments and be lost in the next. Maybe he isn't Miles or Bix or Berrigan, but he's there bringing a bit more life to the streets. Hell, maybe he isn't Roger Woods but some soul-mate successor. But whoever he is, he's there. And he's worth some pocket change. Because maybe some day, you'll hear that one note.

Remembering sergeant and friend who was all Marine

NOT MUCH REMAINS of that special time.

A fatigue cap, washed white-green and hanging forgotten in the back of a closet; relic of a day when it shaded cockier eyes. Marksman's badge. A faded and treasured field jacket with a collar that won't lie flat because it was always yanked up against the wind that blew with cold insistence across air bases from East Texas to Greenland. A thousand fuzzy memories of groping through the maze to manhood. The same war stories we all tell.

And Sgt. Robert J. Beckman, USMC.

For the better part of a year—uneasy at being older and more acutely aware of life's demands—we paraded our military bearing around a small West Virginia college campus. In his case, to the idolatry of the less-seasoned. I rode somewhere in his shadow for a while, envious but comfortable enough with it.

Without the sudden freedom being celebrated by the freshmen all around us, we held fast to a recent past of guard duty and formations in the rain and 72-hour passes. Washed our cars in the dorm parking lot in fatigue pants and jump boots; walked taller than we had since drill instructors goosed us perfectly upright through basic; suffered the sophomoric bull-sessions with tight, amused grins that said, "Sure, kid, but you should've been with us in Marrakesh or Yokohama or Bremen."

The world was our hole card, then, when we felt different.

We silently understood from day one that we were both friends and antagonists. Combatants in endless skirmishing to establish just a sliver of dominance. He was big, curly haired, a face full of charm. Maybe even a little intimidating. And the best of us, then. I was none of that, but somehow insufferably confident. We dueled affectionately in a hundred ways.

"Don't give me that Semper Fi crap," I would tell him on rainy Saturday mornings when we would hole up in the Elkins Moose Club, and drink 3.2 beer and shoot pool and raise a little cautious hell, because we had our image to protect. And, disoriented and put off-balance by that place and time, we'd have died for it.

He was all Marine. Creases in his cords; military press in the blue oxford-cloth shirts; spit-shined cordovans and ramrod swagger. I'd been in a highly trained but route-step outfit and the sloppiness carried over. We never tired of working over that bit of contention.

But I'd put one more year in fatigues than he had, and was stationed for a while with an elite Marine unit, and had been in a place where there was some brief unpleasantness, so I had my edge, too. I nicked him with it when I could, the golden boy.

"Someday I'm going to kick your ass," he would growl when the young college kids were around, worshiping him with their eyes. Truth is, I always thought one day he might and he probably wouldn't have broken a sweat doing it. But it would not have done to admit it. Somehow, we needed that light friction between us; understood that without it, the friendship would sour.

"Uh-huh...*someday*," I'd drawl. "Don't let anything but fear and common sense stop you." And I'd wink at Lenny Rudnick or Frank McDonnell, the other vets on campus, who, if not awed by him, were as impressed as I was.

One night at a fraternity party—the three fraternities courted him shamelessly—he got beered up and took off with the prettiest girl in school. I caught them in the parking lot and demanded his car keys. The girl, gorgeous and on the spoor, protested. He was some catch, Robert J. Beckman was.

"Shut up," he told her.

"The keys."

"Get out of here."

"Give me the damn keys."

What there was between us hung right there.

"Someday," he laughed, staggering back to the party, the sweetheart of Sigma Chi or whatever pouting in his wake.

For everyone, he was the prize. Me, too, I guess.

An old spinster of an English professor favored the four of us—"my veterans" she would coo and then glare at the rest of the class—but she loved him dearly.

"If you all would work as diligently as Mr. Beckman..." she'd lecture. Hell, he hardly studied at all. Like everything else—friendship, girls, frat invitations, beer-chugging, sports—the grades came easily.

Only being different was hard. And we were. For us, the family bond had been broken years before. College was a question mark and challenge. Beyond it, we knew, you would cut it or else. That only threatened three of us. "Got it whipped," he said of the future.

In a semester, he owned the campus as much as any student could. Pledged the preppie fraternity, and oversaw it with bemused indolence. Gave up the Moose for the Coach and Four, a tony restaurant-bar out on the highway where the rich kids from New Jersey gathered. Found his niche, deep and secure.

I was still in search of mine and by spring we had drifted into different places, meeting only occasionally on the lovely campus.

"Hi, flyboy," he'd say. "Hello, jarhead," I would answer. We'd grin. That remained between us.

The next fall I switched schools and years later someone told me he'd gone back into the Marine Corps, this time as an officer. Near the end of the Vietnam War, Capt. Robert J. Beckman was killed in the Mekong Delta.

I guess he has as big a piece of this Memorial day as anyone.

Semper Fi, chum.

His name is etched in that lovely, searing, inky marble. I've been there. Looked up at the name of a young cousin on that wall of individual honor and collective shame; squeezed my eyes closed so hard they still hurt an hour later. Wondered what sort of man the boy who was my cousin might have become. I really didn't know him; Bob Beckman I knew. Four kid veterans long ago, the swagger not yet worn away. A bond. A lesson in the vagaries and varieties of friendship. A reminder of Ecclesiastes...a time to live and a time to die. A man all but shed of a boy's skin...full of promise so rich that only an F. Scott Fitzgerald could've adequately described it. And, then, a name, and a life, etched on a single line. A story told eloquently in just a name. A monument and a place beyond Fitzgerald's literary reach. Someday, I'll go back and look up at that wall, again.

Babe and the bambino: learning the lessons of life

ADAH E. RUSSELL DIED on Sunday. She was, I think, 83. There was never one quite like her, and there never will be.

My Babe.

That's what I called her when I was little and she was taking a major role in raising me while my mother, a worrier, fretted that one or another fatal disaster would befall me before I had cleared the crib.

I would sneeze, my mother laughed in later years, and she'd reach for the phone to call the doctor. "No, he'll be just fine," Babe would say and grease my chest and stuff my nose with the crude oil I can smell to this day.

Babe. The name stuck. Her husband—he was Pop and they lived upstairs all the years I was growing up—even wound up calling her that. All of her friends. I still call the women I like that.

The last time I saw Babe was four years ago. She had lived in Hawaii for years, but was back in Wellsville, Ohio, to visit an ailing sister. Providentially, for me. I was struggling through a hard time then, looking for the assurance that I was the sort of guy I'd always fancied myself to be, and doubting it to my bones. There was small consolation: Babe probably wouldn't have nurtured me all those years if I wasn't salvageable.

"We'll go and see Babe," I told my daughters, suspecting they would find their own reassurance from the woman who had mothered their Dad as much as the grandmother they never knew.

We drove through brilliant sunshine that spring morning, them asking questions, me answering. And remembering, not instances so much, but feelings. Clear back to Babe's kitchen, and, though I always was, never once being told I was "underfoot."

Of sitting next to the stove where she worked with sure movements, and being encouraged to pound the hell out of a bottom of a pot and her just smiling at the racket. Of the time she scratched my back and rubbed ice across my mouth in the long hours after I'd had my tonsils out and my throat was so sore I had assured everyone that I'd probably die by morning. Of the warmth and security and steadiness that she reflected and was as much a part of her as the long, tapering hands and erect carriage and a smile that was ever amused. Of all the times.

Growing up, my girls had shared every memory I'd ever had of Babe and had heard all the stories, but were polite enough to listen to the retelling. The time when I was six and tore my hand wide open on a chain-link fence and wouldn't let anyone even look at it but Babe, because she was a Red Cross nurse during the war and even had a uniform, and I was sure Hippocrates couldn't possibly have known as much about medicine. The way I always behaved for her, because even a cross look would've crushed me and we both understood that, so it never happened. The time her son, Jack, came home during the war, a cocky young fighter pilot, and had challenged her with grinning eyes. She kicked a chair out from under him, a none-too-gentle reminder that if he was all grown up and a war hero, he was also still her son. He calls her Babe, too.

"He was 12 before he knew which one of us was really his mother," my mom always liked to tell people.

My kids never had a Babe, sad to say, but they took to mine. That afternoon in Wellsville, she had said, "You'll be all right. Take care of the girls and be the best you can be." The kids heard something there about their old man, I suspect. Babe had applied yet another bandage.

She did that better than Clara Barton. God, she must've put a hundred of them on me.

"It's OK to cry," she'd say, carefully butterfly-taping a cut closed or washing the dirt from a pavement burn, "but don't move." I would and I wouldn't and, by and by, came to learn two lessons.

Babe got a lot smarter as the years went by with me there under her wing, but still alert for anything adventurous to a boy. "No," my mother would say. "Well, maybe," Babe would decide later, "but be careful." When I wasn't, there she would be.

Babe was a blueprint, I came to understand, for how to be. I remember her teaching me some things, and I remember learning some things from her, and I was a long time understanding the difference.

She fed beggars, and kept the peace in two families that became almost one with easy grace, and once backhanded a mean, full-grown twenty-two-year old for harassing an old man, and cooked the best chicken-and-noodles ever. She could outwork a dray-horse and snatch any of us back in line with a raised eyebrow and sing off-key about as well as anyone you ever heard. She was something.

My Babe.

Once, I was talking about her to a close friend of mine who is a psychologist and he got a got a glint of good humor in his eye. "Must be why you call all the women you love Babe," he said. Must be. In time I've come to understand that men all have a measuring rod for women in their minds. My standard was Babe. They had to have her warmth and her calm and her bemused soul. And when they didn't, or mistakenly I thought they didn't, I eventually moved along. That sounds self-absorbed and insufferable. Maybe even Oedipal. Doubtless it is; it is no less true. If you've been lucky, there has been or is a Babe in your life. To lose one changes you. Leaves you much more alone in the world. A sea anchor suddenly lost in the endless storm. The bitter morning we buried her, I felt more adrift than I ever had. When life became unmanageable, when the pain was too intense and the confusion too great, where would I go? I was a long time knowing that, because of Babe, I could retreat to that home that was me. Yeah, she was something, my Babe.

Al Brandon battled utilities on side of John Q. Public

WHEN Albert D. Brandon shambled into the hereafter Thursday—grudgingly giving way to illness only after a struggle that was long and honorable—those in charge of this commonwealth's public utilities must've heaved a sigh of relief that would've done Mount St. Helens proud.

After almost four decades, Al Brandon's large, capable hands had finally fallen from their necks and the foot he had so often thumped against their hindquarters was still.

Sing low, John Q. Public, there goes the last of the White Knights—what Ralph Nader might've become with a little style. His passing will probably be reflected in your next gas bill.

Across the years, attorney and true consumer advocate Al Brandon fought Bell and Duquesne Light and the railroads and any other utility that raised its head with a passion approaching, if not fury, then the deepest sort of resolution.

The blood usually flowed freely on both sides; Brandon never swung from anywhere but his heels. Oh, he lost his share, but not a stick of furniture was left whole in any courtroom in which he fought.

In a memorable scrap, he lost the major Skybus case in court, but in the process drained away all the public support from it and Skybus died a timely death. It was, he said in high dudgeon, impractical, impossible and too expensive.

Al Brandon was, as he explained once, "vitally angry."

Always at the utilities, always in defense of those who foot the bills. Socrates in a sloppy suit that he wore as though it had been flung upon him from great distance by someone in a hurry.

Tall and loosely gaited, he would pace the courtroom, stopping here and there to lean. He was a great leaner, resting easily against a railing in front of them with a paternal informality which suggested to jurors that, after all, it's us against them, right?

A gray forelock, striped pale yellow from a million clouds of cigarette smoke it absorbed over the years, would scuttle wildly around on his broad forehead and he would alternately bellow his rage at some utility factotum's reluctance or all but whisper in an even tone which implied the sheerest disbelief.

The cliche about looking like an unmade bed could've been coined by anyone who ever saw him. His suits were always too large, his shirts always too small, his ties a technicolor torment. Usually, his glasses were in his hand, deftly leading a witness through his recital or spearing a misleading statement. His wife spent years trying to reform him sartorially and finally gave up.

"He's the kind of a lawyer you see in western movies," a friend once smiled.

Whatever the courtroom style, perhaps that of a rumpled William Jennings Bryan, the message rarely was altered:

These utility people have their hands in our pockets to the elbow and I'm about to remove them, if not by dint of legal brilliance, then by the strength of pure outraged indignation.

Al Brandon was like one of those good-but-not-great light heavy-weights. Sometimes he knocked the other guy stiffer than ice, sometimes they wore him down and got the decision. But he sure did relish the combat.

"I fight all day," he used to say, weariness everywhere on his large, craggy face save for the eyes, which rarely strayed from the jugular of one public utility or the other.

"The utilities grotesquely over-build because their rate base depends on the amount of money they have invested in construction," he would explain from time to time.

In pillorying them, he turned good-natured irascibility into an art form. One time, PAT's John Mauro ended an answer with "sir." Al Brandon smiled. He had a fish.

"Al...it's all right to call me Al, John."

"Al has a cause," said a colleague who knew him well. "He's out to protect the ordinary guy from those who are sure they know what's best for him."

Only Press columnist Roy McHugh, who devoted his first general column in The Press to Brandon and was something of his Boswell, could've put it better.

One day last fall, Brandon called to introduce himself to the new guy in this rectangle and "offer a little help." In semi-retirement at 69, he said he was once more incensed at an old adversary, Ma Bell.

"I know about as much utility law as anyone, although that's among the most modest of claims," he growled in a voice that always sounded like syrup running through gravel.

"Maybe, we could raise a little hell."

That was Al Brandon.

We are, generally speaking, a people in thrall to "characters," those folks we designate by public acclaim over a period of time to be, well, eccentric. Different. Quixotic. Fascinating. Even a little weird. Like that. So taken with them are we that a while back there was a book published entitled "Pittsburgh Characters." Naturally enough, it was written by "Pittsburgh Characters." Al Brandon was perhaps the quintessential Pittsburgh Character. In him, I suspect, was embodied the virtues that we around here most admire about ourselves: mental toughness, grit, a savage delight in tilting with windmills, indomitability and, if and when it is required, physical courage. Al deserved that richest of accolades: he was what the late Art Rooney liked to call "a Pittsburgh guy." Across the decade since Al Brandon's death, no one has surfaced to replace him as the utility companies' menace and the consumer's champion. In fact, no one has even come close.

Klondike caught up in heat of Florida trademark suit

AS PITTSBURGH INSTITUTIONS GO, it ranks right up there with the most meaningful of them all:

Chipped chopped ham. The Gunner screaming through his adenoids, "We had 'em all the way." S'liberty. Kolbassi. The inclines, the bridges, the Democrats, the mills. And, of course, our fealty to that locally hallowed pronoun, yuns'.

But, in a Florida federal court and in supermarket freezers across the country, the Klondike, that great confection of our youth, is under heavy siege. It is the subject of a tough trademark infringement suit.

To some degree, the fate of the Klondike unfortunately is in the hands of a Southern-bred judge who almost surely didn't come of age gnawing on that matchless frozen concoction through the long summer afternoons of his youth.

Man and boy, I have considered the Klondike to be far more than a plain, old square bar of vanilla ice cream, covered with chocolate. Ah, but Shakespeare could not pen words to do it any sort of justice at all.

The ice cream was rich, the way Bill Isaly Sr. and some others made it before it was discovered you could actually produce the stuff without going near a cow's udder. The chocolate would've shamed all of Hershey. Even the silver foil package was as distinctive as the Sistine Chapel ceiling.

Klondikes could be eaten at any time, of course, but they went down best in the heat of summer. On steamy July evenings, my old man liked to sit on the front stoop, another local institution, and munch on one to slowly tease his thirst before walking up to the corner saloon and destroying it with Iron City.

The Isaly stores—there were about a hundred in the Tri-State area before Bill Jr. sold them and put his whole bankroll on the Klondike—were always cool and smelled like a good Kosher deli without the odor of brine.

In most of them, overhead fans of the type found in Shanghai bars churned the air and small boys' imaginations. Large posters depicting Isaly's delicacies dotted the walls. The Skyscraper cone, formed with a silver trowel, offered intrigue. Could the clerk make the two cuts perfectly equal and get the creamy cylinder into the cone on the first try? Or should you have a milk shake? You cannot be said to have lived fully if you have not consumed an Isaly shake, circa 1950. Or the Klondike, which offered elements the others did not. The decision was difficult and usually a matter of basic economics.

But only with old Sam Isaly's invention, brought to glory one 1929 day in his kitchen in Youngstown, Ohio, did you get for your money a variety of matchless pleasures. Biting down on the frozen Klondike gingerly, your front teeth tingling from both the cold and anticipation. The learned skill of eating one neatly, so that the chocolate did not flake off in large pieces, an unsatisfactory occurrence for the purists. Maneuvering the melting bar around in the wrapper to keep your hands, and later your shirt, free of chocolate stains.

Everyone who ate the things had a distinct style. The kid next door, with no thought to his incisors, would immediately bite off a huge chunk and, with terrific will, let it slowly melt on his tongue of its own volition.

My own style was to nibble very evenly, around and around the perimeter, reducing the bar to the size of, oh, a playing card. And then consuming it in one magnificent bite and letting the ice cream that my mouth couldn't contain trickle lazily down my chin.

Klondikes were a soulful experience.

Now, they are under attack by the tentacle of a conglomerate. Kraft Foods, through its Sealtest division, markets an imitator called Polar Bar. It looks like a Klondike, to my way of thinking. It's packaged like a Klondike. It squats in the same frozen food compartments as the Klondike.

But it ain't a Klondike.

The rub is the Sealtest package, which looks to me a whole lot like the Klondike package. Which is why Bill Isaly Jr. spent the last three weeks in a Florida courtroom, where his trademark infringement suit against Kraft is to be decided. A decision isn't expected for some time.

"Our position is that it causes confusion in the marketplace," Isaly was saying yesterday afternoon from his Klondike plant in Clearwater, Fla., from which Klondikes are shipped to 36 states.

Sam Isaly's nephew has been this way before. Kraft is not the first competitor aware that imitation is also the shrewdest form of flattery.

"Frankly, there have been four or five," Bill Isaly says. "They duplicated the silver foil, the tray, the size and shape of the bar, the Arctic cream."

The imitators have not materially damaged the Klondike, the rest of the country apparently possessing the sort of discerning taste that's a hallmark hereabouts.

"We're continuing to grow," Isaly says. "We've shown a 50 percent increase in sales in each of the last three years. By the end of the year, we'll have the Klondike in every state."

This year, the Klondike. Next year, who knows? The entire nation may be reverberating to the cry of "yuns."

To even think of Isaly's is to feel nostalgia bubbling up in the throat. Isaly's was the best ham sandwich ever and Matterhorn ice cream cones and, more than anything, the fabled Klondike and chocolate marking the corners of your mouth. Isaly's was...riding the Pippin', darting and dropping through the Kennywood darkness while remembering that kid of legend who stood up and was decapitated. A '50s tune when rock 'n roll was new and so were many of us, and there was Porky and the Del Vikings and backseat kisses as innocent and sweet as a baby's breath. Isaly's was...and is...a guidepost back to a day when cool was a pack of Luckies rolled into a white T-shirt sleeve and penny loafers, and life was fresh and less-hurried and not at all cheap. The stores are long gone; the time they conjure well past. What remains is nothing more than our longing for both youth and the slow unfolding of time. For Kennywood days and backseat nights. For cobblestone streets and memories worn smooth and romantic by the passing years. Incidentally, Isaly's won its lawsuit, Kraft Foods retreated, and the Klondike is sold from Walla Walla to West Palm. It doesn't taste quite the way it did. Little does.

Parents of girl slain in 1981 still hoping for first clue

THERE IS STILL not a single lead, if there ever was one.

Early one October afternoon in 1981, she was waiting for a bus at Donaldson's Crossroads on Route 19; a bright, likable kid shaking a lifelong shyness and in bloom the way only teen-age girls ever are.

Then, she was gone.

"I dreamt that my child had been abducted and that she had been left unharmed, way out in Missouri or somewhere, and I'd get a call to pick her up," Harry Guenther said while he was waiting and fear was consuming him by the hour.

Five days later, his smiling 15-year-old daughter with the vulnerable eyes and the tomboy ways was found under a pile of leaves.

Since then, nothing.

A large reward for information concerning her death still sits in a bank, mocking all attempts to find any link to her killer. Reporters no longer call. His story, perhaps the saddest one of all, is old. Other teen-age girls have been killed, other parents stricken beyond anyone's understanding. Time has only worn his grief into a different shape.

A man who knows Harry Guenther says carefully, "He wasn't himself for a very long time."

Christine Guenther has been dead 29 months now and there is only one real hope left to her father: Another rehashing of the Guenthers' tragedy. Another chance that someone, somewhere, will remember something. Another newspaper story.

Maybe it will kick free a memory in one mind of someone or something unusual around Donaldson's Crossroads that afternoon. Maybe someone will remember an unguarded statement. Killers often brag, the cops say. Maybe someone will recall something. Maybe.

The last time anyone saw Christine Guenther alive was on Oct. 26, 1981. She was two miles from her Peters Twp. home, waiting for a bus to take her to the doctor's.

She was a pretty kid with a heart-shaped face and a thin smile that, in one newspaper photograph anyway, implied some instinctive wryness. A sophomore at Peters Twp. High School. Cocked her head just so in embarrassment at the camera. Big eyes full of good nature; 5-5, with that stockiness young girls often have when they play tennis and swim and ski and don't mine being called a jock.

She was wearing blue cords, a navy blue sweater over a light-blue blouse. And maybe a puzzled look, because she'd been waiting for the bus on the wrong corner.

That afternoon, she vanished. A hunter found her in a patch of South Fayette Twp. woods. The principal at Peters Twp., John Shafer, was talking about Christine's school friends later, but he said it for a lot of others:

"They will always remember. This wasn't understandable to us. She was such a nice girl. There was just no rhyme or reason to it."

None that was apparent. No sexual attack. No robbery. She still had three dollar-bills when she was found. Her father works for the United Steelworkers, but the cops quickly ruled out any connection. Just a senseless, unfathomable killing of a young girl who several people described as "wonderful."

What remains now is pain, and the reward, and maybe 1,500 people who've reached out in some way to Harry and Carmen Guenther. And a father wanting his daughter's killer found to put some sort of punctuation behind his grief.

"There were a few early calls, from people just wanting the money," he was saying yesterday. "It's not practical for the fund to go on indefinitely. But we'll consult with the police before we disband it."

Four funds, actually. Totaling more than $30,000 in reward money. You know the words...for information leading to the arrest and conviction...Still, there has never been a solid contact.

Oh, local police want to talk to Texas cops holding a mass murderer who says he killed more than 100 women in 16 states. "An interview has to be scheduled months in advance, so many agencies want to talk to this guy," Harry Guenther sighs.

Otherwise, there is very little:

An organization the Guenthers began as a support system for parents who'd been through a similar crucible —"she'd want some good to come out of this," Carmen Guenther says of her daughter.

And the reward funds that have failed to raise even a single lead, or any that Harry Guenther has heard about: "The worst person they could ever tell they had a suspect is me."

And one more newspaper story.

Occasionally, you write about their tragedies and they become friends. It was that way with Harry and Carmen. They aren't together now; haven't been since a few years after their daughter's death. Neither live anywhere near Donaldson's Crossroads, although, ironically enough, I am writing these words just a few miles from there. In time, the wry humor that has always been his trademark slowly crept back into Harry Guenther's ice-blue eyes. Still, it fights for space with a chronic sadness. Carmen's personal signature is in her quick, easy smile. It is engaging enough that in the late 1980s, she almost rode it into a seat on the Pittsburgh City Council. Intelligence and honesty foiled her candidacy. There is beauty in her face; sometimes it is unshadowed. The loss of a child of innocence benumbs many parents; traps them there in an inconsolable grief for the remainder of their days. Harry and Carmen fought their way free. At a cost known only to them. They remain what they were before that early October day 13 years ago: what we mean when we use the term "good people." Christine's killer has not been found.

On teen-age dining patterns, the doctor knows less

I FIGURE I'VE killed off 100 or so Chinese kids in my lifetime
That was by my old man's reckoning. "Eat everything on your plate" was
the edict in our house when I was growing up. The reason, of course, was
obvious: "Millions of children are starving to death in China."

The logic always eluded me—I couldn't figure how he planned to get my
uneaten spaghetti to Peking before it spoiled—but on the issue of plate-clean-
ing, my father brooked no discussion. When dinner was over, the plates
could've bypassed the sink and gone directly from the table to the cupboard,
so spotless were they.

But, whatever their other evils, the communists seemed to have resolved
the age-old problem of starving Chinese kids and now along comes Dr. John
Greene from Vanderbilt University to state unequivocally that eating everything on the plate is bad for kids and some other things which makes me wonder after his credentials.

Greene is reputedly a specialist in adolescent eating disorders, which in
our house come in every variety from the kid who nibbles the placemats if
dinner is late, to one who thinks the apex in epicurean delight is a frozen veal
pattie, to one who seems to subsist on M&Ms, lemon-lime Kool-Aid, vitamins
and whatever diet has captured the fancy of the editors of Seventeen magazine.

Greene contends that generally we parents misuse food as it applies to children and advises not to tell kids to clean their plates, or send them to bed without dinner when they misbehave, or suggest they eat something sweet after a
bad day at school, "to make them feel better."

Doing any of the above, he explains, can result in teen-age eating disorders,
by which I take it he means grocery bills the size of the Zambian Gross
National Product. But I suspect Greene may spend too much time in academia,
poring over statistics, and not enough in the nation's dining rooms.

Had he been in mine Saturday, for example, he would've discovered no
particular evidence to support his theories, which seem to run diametrically
opposed to my own observations.

The Lady otherwise occupied, I selected the menu with an eye toward sim-
plicity and quantity—hot dogs, baked beans, and those leftovers in the refrigerator which did not need shaved.

"What's for dinner?" inquired Kevin, an 11-year-old who from the navel
down is hollow.

"Beans and hot dogs."

"Yuk."

"How many hot dogs do you want?" I asked.

"Four."

"Kyle?"

"Four."

The competitive streak in 13-year-old Kyle is four lanes wide.

"Five," he reconsidered. "I could eat six if you want."

It would no doubt revolt Greene to know that five boys ages 9 to 15 consumed 23 hot dogs, with buns, two of the largest-size cans of baked beans that Campbell's has on the market, and enough other comestibles to ward off malnutrition in Bangladesh for a week.

Greene worries that children will get fat.

"Eighty percent of obese adolescents carry their excess weight into adulthood," he warns.

Uh-huh. Obese adolescent, in my experience, is largely a contradiction in terms. Of the aforementioned kids, it would easily be possible to take a pair of drumsticks and tap out "Life Is Just A Bowl Of Cherries" in 4/4 time on their rib cages.

Greene also observes that adolescence is a propitious time to straighten out the eating habits of teenagers because they are extremely conscious of their bodies and want to be attractive to their peers.

"I think I'm anorexic," 15-year-old Kari has announced about hourly since she discovered the opposite sex a couple of years and 73 swains back. If the term hour-glass figure had not been coined long ago, it would have been by the first teen-age boy to see her at the local pool.

Finally, Greene totally abandons reality. Tell kids to eat slowly, he advises. This is the rarest sort of foolishness. There is not a parent alive who doesn't know that the average kid can consume a seven-course meal in the time it takes an adult to belch.

The standard measures for speed should be changed from miles-per-hour or revolutions-per-minute to some sort of barometer dealing with the given time it takes a kid's fork to make it from his plate to his mouth.

But Greene most reveals his lack of insight with the recommendation that children should not be allowed to eat while watching television. That's what probably led to all those starving Chinese kids.

And who has ever seen Hill Street Blues through anything but a peanut-butter haze?

It has been both my torment and my secret delight to have seen to the feeding of any number of children. In spite of Dr. Greene's theories and my own sloth in front of the stove, all of those children have apparently thrived on my food preparation. Or, at least, their growth was not noticeably stunted. They are all full-grown, Kyle and Kevin Moon big men, and their sister, Kari, easily strong enough to have borne a child. My crowning kitchen achievement, however, is Samnoun Srun, who recently graduated from high school, also has achieved full size, and was there for a long while the untitled World-Champion Eater. A brief anecdote. Once when eight-year old

Samnoun was eating his way through the family budget, I suggested a serious wager to Pittsburgh restaurateur Steve (Froggy) Morris. I would bet $100 that my kid, who then weighed perhaps 85 pounds, could out-eat a friend of Froggy's named Big Bubba, who tipped the scales at a delicate 520 pounds. When I described Samnoun's daily intake, Morris abruptly declined the bet. I have no credentials in the area of nutrition, of course, but I do have a considerable body of anecdotal evidence to support my contention: Let them eat what they want, when they want, and feed them lots of hot dogs and baked beans. That way, they will like you better, grow up without indigestion, and perhaps even take care of you in your old age. But don't forget the vitamins.

Original Oyster House draws the man as it did the boy

I STILL GO BACK, occasionally.

To watch the people. A red-nosed stew bum clutching a shot of Imperial in unsteady hands, squeezing cheek-by-cheek next to a kid stockbroker in blue blazer, rep tie and widening eyes.

To look at the fight pictures hung at random all over the faded walls, Ezzard Charles left-hooking Jersey Joe Walcott's nose under his ear.

To hear the sounds heard nowhere else. Crowd noise, loud and jangling, but without anger, and as much a part of the place as the smell of frying fish. The belly laughter from working men hunched over the scarred, mahogany bar. The dumbwaiter groaning and wheezing down from the kitchen. "Fish up!...Yessir, oyster-and-a-buttermilk, coming right up...need some hot sauce here..."no, lady, we don't have hamburgers..."

To eat. The fish sandwiches, so good they would've land-locked Ahab. A form of ambrosia. Nightingales fluttering across your tongue.

To drink a draft or two and remember the days when they would've tasted so much colder and held the sweet, sweet flavor of forbidden fruit.

The Original Oyster House in Market Square. What the Orient Express might've become if it had been stationary and served whiskey-with-a-buttermilk-chaser.

There it has squatted for forever on the corner of an alley, like a tired, proud, old middleweight, daring pedestrians to enter and time to inflict anything more than scar tissue.

Forget those seven other tawdry impostors you can find in various malls around the area. Hell, they don't even have white hexagonal ceramic tiles on the floor, or pictures of the Miss America field for four decades on the walls, or the mandatory bag lady, propped crookedly in a wooden ice-cream chair and slowly gumming a breaded oyster next to a couple of kids with zits trying to hustle the waiter into serving them beer.

Yeah, for me the place is a Capistrano. Small bites of my youth were spent in the place and the man is no less intrigued.

Some of the best of it has faded, sad to say. Old Tom, the grouch of a waiter who conducted guerrilla warfare against the bartenders and the customers with equal relish, has gone. As has his colleague, George, the ex-wrestler who didn't think the service was correct unless he put his thumb in what you were drinking.

"He'd stick his fingers in the glasses on the way to the tables," laughs owner Lou Grippo, "and I'd scream at him.

"He'd say, 'Listen, I been doing it this way for 20 years and until I get a complaint, I'm going to keep doing it.'"

Old Tom and George have gone and now even the big sandwich is different, even if only a bit less than it was in its heyday when I was 15 and snarling back at Old Tom as a respected customer was honor-bound to do. Grippo says it isn't his fault and I believe him. Forgiveness, of course, is out of the question.

Japan cornered the market on the South African cold-water whiting Lou used to use, and he won't buy the warm-water stuff that comes form South American waters.

"Too many bones and they don't clean it right," he grouses, having switched to cod.

The McKees Rocks bakery that made the delicious oversized buns went out of business and even Grippo buying a piece of a bakery in Altoona couldn't resolve the problem. So the new buns are the standard-sized 5 to 6 inches, instead of the old heavyweights that were marginally smaller than manhole covers.

Still, I am lured back almost as often as when I was a kid looking guiltier than sin.

"Fish-and-a-draft," I would softly demand, eyes down, breath held.

"Yes, one *root* beer," Old Tom would sneer and shuffle three feet to the bar, roughly shouldering his way between customers hovering around his station and growling at the bartenders who dealt the food.

"The clientele at the Downtown store has changed," says Grippo, who has changed with it swiftly and surely enough that he owns eight Oyster Houses and spent yesterday interviewing prospective managers for a couple of new places he plans to open. "We used to get mostly blue-collar. And the sports crowd. Newspaper guys and numbers writers."

Hmmmmn.

These newer customers, though, don't know a thing. Last time I was in the Fish House—that's what I called it as a kid and that's how I still think of it—I heard a guy ask for tartar sauce. Probably puts chocolate syrup on asparagus, too.

"When I bought the place, I couldn't believe they didn't serve ketchup," Lou Grippo says. But what does he know? Only the uncivilized would put ketchup on his fish.

No, an Oyster House fish sandwich—Grippo has only owned the place since 1970 and is merely an entrepreneur—requires only four items.

Salt: sprinkled a bit lavishly because the fish is not puny and easily handles seasoning.

Hot sauce: don't splash it unevenly like a klutz, but spill the red dots with some precision.

The clear liquid in the white glass bottle: white vinegar with little green chilies chopped in it and some whole red ones for color.

An appreciation of perfection.

Sonny, in whose shadow I walked through my teens, liked the breaded oysters best. A pearl of shellfish in a sea of french-fried dough. Buttermilk, with the shiny, yellow slivers flickering, on the side. I'm still a fish-and-a-beer guy. Yeah, deep into our 50s now, we still return to the Fish House, in search of a slice of what we were. Place hasn't changed much, other than what was noted above. Expansion to the shopping malls didn't work. Food was still the same, but the ambience was lousy. No bag ladies; smiling teenyboppers rather than the gnarly old men who threw the stuff at you Downtown in a way that said, "yeah...you're lucky to be here!" But the original still stands in Market Square...a tired, old prize-fighter with enough left to sting the fast-food joints. Somebody famous comes to town, they still get hauled off to have their picture taken in the Original Oyster House and join Sinatra and Joe Louis and the Miss America girls on the crowded walls. Outside on the wall, a plaque informs passersby that the building is an Historic landmark, as if they didn't know. The Jenkins Arcade...Syria Mosque...other places woven so tightly into the fabric of Pittsburgh have disappeared. Sacrificed to a false god, something called "progress." The Oyster House remains, testimony that hereabouts we cherish at least some of our history and our lore. The suburban imitators are dead. Long live the Original Oyster House.

To Old Man, Democratic race would've been a crawl

THIS PENNSYLVANIA PRIMARY ENCOUNTER— a timid confrontation mindful of a pillow fight in a senior citizens center—would've been painful for the Old Man. He liked his politics as he did his steak: blood rare.

Upon entering the gates of heaven, the Old Man was certain, Democrats weren't even required to slow down. Republicans, of course—those with good sense, anyway—never approached the place.

To his marrow, he was a Jacksonian Democrat, with populist overtones. A man to whom politics meant passion. Mondale, Hart and Jesse Jackson, it is suspected, would've inspired him to spit. One, a puppet, tugged to and fro by a thousand strings. Another, a glib Westerner with a wispy slogan and no respect for the hard lessons history has taught those of us living here in the real world. And the third, sweet Lord, a preacher who'd seemingly be most at ease at a used-car lot.

It might've been enough to drive the Old Man, who did not believe in campaign flesh wounds, to switch his party affiliation.

That's probably an overstatement, though. To his flinty core, the Old Man believed that Republicanism was, if not the tool of the devil, surely a form of virulent disease. Republicans, all the generations of them that he'd known or read about, failed to grasp a simple fact of political life: Government is simply a methodology for bettering the lives of the people. Not to be feared, but to be used down to the nub.

"And anyone who doesn't understand that, boy, does not read...or is a fool," he would say on those long summer afternoons in the years when he was entrusted to oversee my education in such diverse elements as politics and trout fishing. He had credentials for both.

He had—he swore proudly and fiercely to his death at 87 of terminal tedium brought on by a broken hip that defied mending—published the very first "truly Democratic newspaper West of the Alleghenies." One governor of this commonwealth listed the Old Man on the gubernatorial stationery as one of his three formal advisers.

The Old Man would not have been amused by Walter Mondale or Gary Hart or Jesse Jackson. Although, in the case of the latter, he always did mightily admire a rogue with charm.

"Scalawags," he would call them, but with just a hint of sparkle in tired eyes that glinted with intelligence and scorn and a defiant awareness that he was in his winter.

Democrats got to be scalawags; Republicans were scoundrels. There was, he would bitingly observe, considerable difference.

The Old Man had no truck with the posturing so prevalent in the state this past week, or those who failed to view the political process as he did: As the grandest of all games; played willingly in the muck and mud; no mercy offered, none sought; the Marquis of Queensberry a conspicuous absentee.

"A dirty business," he would say in a tone others reserved for ordering strawberry shortcake.

Gary Hart, he would've shunned. If for nothing more than his feeble attempt—"Nobody owns me!"—at independence. Presidential politics, the Old Man thought, was not so much the art of compromise, but the art of manipulation, by whatever means were at hand. The Old Man favored the stick.

Generations ago, he once forced a state legislator into resigning by the simple means of constantly referring to the man editorially as: "A liar and a thief and, worse, a fool."

"There weren't any libel laws, then," he explained some years later.

Mondale, the Old Man probably would've accorded a certain respect, built of party loyalty, but Fritz would've lost it and gained a bitter enemy long before today's primary.

"A tough, tough couple of months," Mondale groaned here the other day.

The Old Man thought tough was what you made it on your enemies.

"You yank on that hook, boy, it'll hurt a whole lot worse," he would say, and then push the barb firmly through your finger and go looking for the wire cutters.

Jesse Jackson would have, after being nearly lashed to death by invective, won the Old Man's grudging editorial support. He favored the underdog—"nobody tries too hard to buy them and so they come to office with minimal campaign obligations"—and he would've enjoyed the preacherman's resolution under the fire generated by his "Hymie" remark.

No doubt, though, the Old Man would've observed that it's a very short step from "Hymie" to "Honkie," a fact which has escaped most political pundits.

Mostly, the Old Man would've railed at this primary campaign's bloodlessness. Its grayness and blandness. Mondale and Hart pelting each other with spitballs; Jackson holding their coats and raining impotent criticism on them from a safe distance. Mondale's swaying in the breeze of Hart's back-stretch rush. Hart's vacuousness and lack of killer instinct. Jackson's gaffes.

Going to the polls this day, he would've saved for each of them his bitterest indictment: "Worse than Republicans."

He was, by trade, a printer. And when he had pushed well into his 80's, he routinely worked 12-hour days and could set 6-point type in a hand-held stick so quickly the movement of his hands made a blur in the air. At nine, he was apprenticed as what used to be called a "printer's devil," or helper. Some 75 years later, he said he was still "learning the trade."

At times, he owned newspapers that cut the corrupt men of his day like a lash. In the early 1930s, when the town of Wilkinsburg was owned by such men, he rented a biplane and dumped thousands of flyers calling for reform over that "City of Churches." He was arrested and spent almost a week in jail because he refused to post bond as a matter of principle. One time a crew repairing a streetcar line in front of his home at 4 a.m. refused to shutdown a noisy compressor. The Old Man went in the house, got his .12 gauge, and blew up the compressor. They jailed him for that, too.

He was my most unforgettable character.

A Little Chip Off The Old Block Goes With The Grain

CARRY A POINTED stick in all dealings with politicians, bankers, public officials and others of debatable character...consider carefully what injures, inspires, angers and amuses the readers, whose wine you drink and whose song you had damn well better sing...keep a sharp eye on Republicans and preachers...and don't take yourself seriously, nobody else figures to...

Those, then, would be the silent marching orders I received yesterday from The Old Man—whose boy I have not been for some long time. So, by way of introduction to me, a scant chip, you get him, the block gone but never quite absent. The thought here is that you be forewarned; much of The Old Man remains in what used to be the boy.

I couldn't quit thinking of him on my first day back at The Press. A quarter-century back, at 87, boredom and a busted hip that resisted healing finally conspired to kill him after considerable struggle; still, he lingers:

His wit, to a boy often gruff and wounding. "I hooked this big trout, but..." Distracted, his gaze would shift out over the valley. "Can't eat a broken leader, boy." His scholarly bent, palpable opinions on history and politics and current events flaking from his mind in large bites that choked me, and still do. His ideals, equally large and indigestible. His dreams and schemes—quickly sacrificed to some project suddenly more alluring.

Clearing a mountainside one summer and having a huge flag painted on it and spotlighted, so it could be seen for 20 miles. Animals could not be deterred from eating the spotlight's wiring. After that, he carried a .22 and no varmint ever saw him before it was too late. A lake to attract migrating Canadian geese—the flyway turned out to run through the next county. A mountaintop, leveled for a forest of rose bushes that didn't survive June. A pair of Jersey calves that were to be the nucleus of his new beef herd. Two heifers, as it turned out, which he later had to lure up a plank and onto a truck that carried them off to a slaughterhouse. He stayed gone from the house till dark that night.

A flinty old man of vision; sadly enough, a bit myopic. But I digress. He had always advised approaching serious work the way he did my grandmother when she was, as he would say, "gingery." So, wandering about yesterday in the very large shoes left by Roy McHugh, I did the prudent thing and went out in search of decent coffee and an answer to the question of how best to write a first column. Which is much like a first affair—to be briefly relished and then done with, if only for its awkwardness.

The day before, I'd fed a banquet of bloodworms to a couple of seasoned trout and mused over both my initial effort as McHugh's repl...successor and how The Old Man might view me abandoning sports for the real world. With jaundice, I suspect, but not without a certain satisfaction.

He was a newspaperman off and on for the better part of 70 years and only my grandmother's sweetness, Marsh Wheeling cigars, aged Kentucky whisky and his place in the mountains meant more to him than the business which provided him with a rostrum from which to dole out wrath, insight, revelation and occasional praise. Which he was wont to toss about as though it consisted of large-denomination bills.

I still remember the lead to one column he wrote before freshly-minted libel laws snatched him, squirming, into responsibility. "That renowned jackal, Mayor Atkinson, yesterday approved a heinous plan to..."

As a coltish adolescent, I summered with The Old Man, lunging after his grudging approval, wondering over his eccentricity, and mostly suffering the grouchiness of his 70s with the tractability of youth. In him, I can increasingly see me. In time, it is hoped you will forgive us both our sins.

Those summers that I was allowed to roam within the boundaries of The Old Man's watchful gaze, I fished in silvery creeks for fat, feisty trout and his reluctant approval. His affection..."Boy, you've grown two inches this summer..." could make me a foot taller. Inching uncertainly toward manhood, his strong opinions rang in my ears. They have formed the base for many of mine, which you are now called upon to suffer or dismiss, the latter course to be recommended on occasion.

The Old Man held with a lot of self-evident truths:

Republicans should be buried vertically, as to waste as little of the good earth as possible; their virtues largely stemming from having made enough money to forgo the need of plundering the public purse. A grand, old Democratic tradition, he liked to note. The only worthwhile Democrats could trace their fealty straight back to Jefferson and Jackson with no deviationist stops along the way.

But Democrats made far the best rogues and he would've treasured Cyril Wecht, all the while pillorying him. Government, he insisted, is just a tool and only fools are fearful of using it for the general good. Bankers are to be scrutinized because many would steal your stove and return an hour later for the smoke. And, above all else, in the natural order of things, clerics, lawyers and physicians fall somewhere far to the South of newspapermen—to whom everyone alive must one day surely have to answer.

He always said what he meant in a loud voice, lest his opinions confuse a single soul. Which, incidentally, he held small hope for any deity retrieving. Still, it was his command to revere women for their warmth, small children for their malleability as well as their affection, animals for their devotion, and the rest of us for whatever minute promise we might hold.

A life-long Democrat, he was said to have formally advised a couple of governors. Often to do their constituents a favor and resign office as quickly as humanly possible.

Some of The Old Man will creep into this rectangle from time to time, I'm afraid. Again, forewarned is forearmed.

The Old Man was, of course, my grandfather. Bert M. Musick. Short of stature, long on passionately-held beliefs. Elsewhere in these pages, you will find other reflections on him, and us.

I tend to think a lot about him lately, having not long ago become a rookie grandfather, myself. The business of grandfathering seems easy enough. As I can best understand it, it calls for: The dispensing of affection, keeping your mouth shut when matters of discipline are being discussed, the willingness to perform any number of small chores having to do with lifting and bending, pointing out interesting things to look at, providing a lap when necessary or desirable, buying ice cream, discreetly removing dangerous objects from a child's path, and not making much noise when a small shoe collides with your groin.

I think I do tolerably well at it. As I said, it's easy enough. In fact, I hope to do a lot more of it.

Personal Magic Turns Him Into
The Prince Of The Bar Scene

FROGGY MORRIS is opening a couple of new saloons, which will come as good news to any number of distilleries, the antsier singles, those with decent expense accounts, the manufacturer of Bromo-Seltzer and Dr. Thomas Starzl. Alcoholics Anonymous, of course, is trembling at the prospect.

Morris is a 38-year-old saloonkeeper with considerable heft, a voice that conjures a ton of anthracite scuttling down a tin coal chute, and the touch of Croesus on a cash register he has been playing like Basie for almost four years.

Drinking in his place as a regular is guaranteed to give you hip-pointers, a liver the size and elasticity of a catcher's mitt, and an address book larger than the Yellow Pages.

The day before Thanksgiving of 1979, Morris opened the doors to Froggy's on Market Street and had to leap back to avoid being splattered against the wall. Business has pretty much stayed that way since, his joint a trendy hangout for men of any and all descriptions and a lot of lacquered women with eyes that hint of sin.

"I want them all," he rasps, the voice which gave him his nickname creating a noise suggestive of gargling with ground glass. "I don't care who they are. I've had the U.S. Attorney and the biggest bookmaker in town standing next to each other at that bar."

He waves vaguely toward the polished mahogany, where a relaxed mid-afternoon crowd of serious drinkers ignores responsibility in favor of booze, conviviality, and the chance of getting a phone number. A stunning girl in leather blows cigarette smoke in the face of an overeager guy in a Madras sports jacket that ought to be covering some lawn furniture.

The food is decent enough in Morris's place; the drinks high-priced and damn near paralyzing; and the ambiance equal parts brass, ferns, sports memorabilia, lazily revolving ceiling fans, airiness, and people hitting on one another.

In toto, there are showier and tonier places in this town to drink, but they come to mind very slowly. Froggy, then, has the touch, even though business is slowing from the previous feverish pace and awaits rekindling in his newest establishments.

On this fine afternoon, glaring over his shoulder at a woman with a bawling baby—"Bringing kids in bars, I hate that!"—Froggy Morris slouches on a chair in a far corner of his establishment and considers various inquiries:

Why has he become a local institution, fitting in there someplace between Irish politicians voting corpses and the nasally pronoun "yuns?" And why is he able to sustain lines outside Froggy's while his major competitors, to a saloon, have been shooting stars? And, essentially, what makes Froggy Morris run?

"I'm opening a new joint," Morris huffs, wiping sweat from a face you would buy a used car from only in desperation. "I'm running my buns off."

Which he is wont to do. Froggy's begat Froggy's Roadhouse in Mt. Lebanon, which will open in late September and begat Froggy's Dogs & Deli, which will grace the new PPG Building and further increase his stature as a purveyor of spirits.

It stems, one suspects, largely from Morris's personality. Which is mostly that of an amiable walrus—he sports a mustache that strains his coffee—given to bellowing at but never ignoring the customers, who are known affectionately as "bums."

That he can address them as such and still do crisp business, Morris attributes to: his help, preppily dressed and as courteous as footmen; his drinks, expensive but easily capable of knocking down a grown man, and his food, of which he boasts, one suspects, more than the clientele. Still for a Rochester, N.Y., native who swapped law school for liquor and had to be bodily thrust into Pitt by his father, Steve Morris had done handsomely by himself.

"It took off almost at the start," he says of business, "but the next September, we opened the upstairs and it exploded."

Now, it merely crackles resoundingly, but Morris is unconcerned.

"Only a fool would think you could sustain it," he says. "New places open, some customers get bored. You give them their money's worth, you treat them right, you'll do business."

You may even do business at more than one location, which Morris will shortly be doing, even if he isn't quite sure why.

"The money's not so important," he says. "It's the action that intrigues me."

Action always has. Following high school, Morris "went around the world, literally," as an itinerant seaman. His father permitted such foolishness until Morris returned home briefly only to announce he was bound for the site of a recent earthquake.

"You're not going to any earthquake," thundered Morris Sr. "You are going to college."

Morris went to Pitt and later lasted through four months of law school—"I resigned before they resigned for me." The judicial system's loss was the world of liquor's gain and Morris quickly acquired his nom d'affaires.

"I figured out very early in the game that you got drunks out the door easier by yelling at them than by smacking them," he says. "One night, a guy says, 'Hey, Froggy, take it easy!' It stuck."

So, too, has its owner.

Froggy's idling there in brass and polished hardwood splendor on Market between the Blvd. of the Allies and First Avenue, is the finest saloon in the world. I state that unequivocally and as a guy who, until a few years ago, did exhaustive research on the subject.

Why it is without serious competition as a place to drink, I am less sure. It has something to do with those who work there and in some sense, the awareness that they take a more than a proprietary interest in what goes on. Duffy, the day bartender who has been with Morris from the beginning, never hesitates to make sport of the boss. One day, having just gone off both booze and cigarettes in the same instant and being in a querulous mood, Duff answered a Morris' phone call thusly: "Can't talk to you, I'm swamped." At the moment, I was the only customer in the place.

Ron Wallace is the manager. Probably the only saloon pro with a master's degree in Fine Arts from Columbia University. He will listen to Morris' business decisions somewhat respectfully, nodding where appropriate, then do what he wants to.

Certainly, Steve Morris' saloon-operating acumen and gruff, garrulous personality have much to do with the fact that few joints, anywhere, have been as consistently successful.

He is what we around here mean when we speak of "characters." As in people who are different and singular. Once I was at the bar when he consummated a business deal with a guy whose eyes were never still. He bought 10,000 watches for a dollar apiece, and later sold some and gave away the rest as though they were packs of matches.

Morris' friends, which is to say a lot of his customers, are diverse. One night, I sat at the bar between a man who had recently been nominated to the federal judiciary and a guy whose title could best be described as "Capo."

People who wouldn't brag about being on a first-name basis with the Pope airily announce, "Froggy Morris in a friend of mine."

Frog's Dogs and Deli and The Roadhouse didn't stand the test of time. There wasn't enough of the proprietor to go around.

The Gutter's Dining On Doughnuts
While The Band Plays On

"OH, SAY can you see...what so proudly we hailed...?"

It is dinner time. He and some knowing pigeons wait under the Downtown street light he calls home.

Eddie is late. But not as late the other regulars, Coat Lady and The Witch. His only competition this night will be the pigeons.

He rips open the garbage bag, removes a day-old doughnut. Liquid pours from it and over his hands. He touches a fingertip to it, tastes, licks the doughnut. Coffee, not the rancid cooking grease.

Outmaneuvering the pigeons is easy. When he hasn't been "to Purgatory" for a few hours, he's always too quick for the birds. When the cheap muscatel slows him, he shares. Evolution restricts them to pecking; he eats a doughnut in one bite.

The bag is half-full of stale pastries. A young red-haired woman had brought his meal straightaway, just before 6 p.m., to the alley that runs a half-block and another world off Liberty Avenue.

"He'p you with that," he had offered, deftly relieving her of two plastic trash bags and heaving them back up the alley, dropping them heavily, but falling lightly beside them. Both are gutted by a finger, the one holding coffee grounds shoved aside.

He is hungry. So are the pigeons. He shoos them away, wolfing a doughnut, the birds fluttering at his flanks for crumbs.

"...o'er the ramparts we watched were so gallantly streaming..."

Man does not live by bread alone. He roots deeper into one of the plastic bags and locates a tall soup can that he knows by experience will be there. LeGout brand cream of chicken, the dregs congealing in the bottom. He drains it, noisily spitting out some coffee grains.

A fat, graying woman teeters past the alley opening and jerks her head toward the sound. He pays her no mind, roots some more. The heat in the alley wafts a cloud of decay toward the avenue. Sight and smell freeze the fat woman for a long moment before she scuttles away. The stench will stay in her nose for blocks.

But he has not time for the passers-by. They stop briefly; he knows embarrassment will move them on quickly. Unless he is bumming change for the wine, he ignores them. And dinner must now give way to commerce.

Fed, he prods the garbage bag in earnest now, loading discarded cartons with old doughnuts and trundling to the curb and a large cardboard box.

"Damn, can't find nothin'," he snuffles to no one, wiping his nose on the stained green raincoat which drags at his heels. Under it, a heavy red sweater and a girls' red vinyl rain-jacket squeeze his neck into fat folds. He hopes no one has stolen his winter coat, which is rolled up and hidden in his kip, a large bush in a nearby park.

"There's a lot of them around here," says a watchman in an office building next to the doughnut place. "They sleep all over."

"In the winter...?"

The watchman shrugs.

In the alley, mumbling can be heard.

"I believe in both candidates. Good men. Don't exactly know which way I'll go, yet." Memories shake the head bent over garbage. "I believe the man gave me a break. No, I don't think he 'tended to hurt me. Believe he giving me a break." For a while, he talks about the police dogs he owns, and "bein' kin to Reagan."

From the motherlode, he yanks two large doughnuts out of the trash and holds them to the light streaming down the alley, studying them the way a jeweler might an emerald. He pokes one with a finger.

"Apple!" he decides. The jewels go into the cardboard box beside a gallon bottle that holds a teaspoon of Open Pit barbecue sauce; a partially eaten roll; more LeGout cans; a carton with a thick, brown liquid drying on the sides, and his white envelopes.

They are his treasures. In the doughnut joint, he often goes into a corner and hides them from the girls. "They're full of dirt," the girls laugh later.

On this warm evening, the trash bag emptied, his own leavings carefully placed in a dumpster, his box now loaded, he leaves the alley. Somebody on the street, he knows, will pay a nickel, maybe a dime, for a few doughnuts. Then, "I'll be goin' to Purgatory..."

"Oh! say does that star-spangled banner yet wave..."

Coat Lady, who wears several in all weather, and The Witch, who swears at passers-by and is mannish and mean, are no-shows. The doughnut girls are surprised. "They're always here...this is their meeting place. They say this is their home."

In minutes, Eddie returns to his home under the street light, the cardboard box hidden in another alley.

"I'm used to eating three, four meals a day," he explains to a passer-by, "and a snack."

Someone once said, "I'm for whatever gets you through the night, Jesus Christ or Jack Daniels." A buck changes hands. There are worse places than Purgatory.

Twilight takes over Liberty Avenue as he leaves. One of the girls from the doughnut joint starts home. "It's kind of sad," she decides. "But they let themselves get like that."

"...o'er the land of the free and the home of the brave."

One morning, Eddie just disappeared. The girls in Dunkin' Donuts never saw him, again. A few years later, Purgatory, the winos' heaven farther along Liberty Avenue, closed its doors.

I spent a couple of hours one day a month or so afterwards trying to find out what became of old Eddie. The social worker at St. Mary's, the Downtown sanctuary for the street people, didn't know.

"If he's the man I'm thinking of, I didn't even know his name was Eddie," she said. "There are a lot of Eddies." So there are. Occasionally, I still see the Coat Lady.

The Maulers: A Nickname Which Is Unmistakably Suitable

MAULERS? Damn straight, as we say around here, or used to. Maulers!

Has the fine, crisp ring of a streetcar running over exposed shins. Sternums shattering in the sunshine. Pillaging and rapine. Sudden violence up a midnight alley.

Unsuitable for squash, surely. Or for any athletic entity representing, say, Paris or Beverly Hills. But here, as appropriate as a flapping window on a PAT bus.

Granted, it wants a bit of getting used to, but ultimately it will play in a place where the iron imperative is getting it done. Where, when men bump one another on the street, they usually ignore "pardon me," in favor of "watch it, Mac!"

Webster defines the word maul as having to do with a heavy hammer, or mace, which locally is an instrument used mostly by ward chairmen on the pocketbooks of payrollers. A secondary definition—"to injure by a rough beating" is, of course, what the Steelers have been about for some time.

While Maulers lacks a certain sharp authority—Flailers? Flagellants? Bashers?—the inspirational message is unmistakable. And, as the redoubtable Carroll H. Cook was telling a caller yesterday afternoon, "It's a lot better than Flash. Anyone does a flashing job around here, they get...mauled."

So the city's freshly caught United States Football League club will enter the lists as the Maulers, the choice bearing both the imprimatur and general interest of owner Ed DeBartolo, who builds maul...shopping centers and lends money to the Rockefellers.

He favored the name over such wimpy possibilities as the Renaissance, Points and Flash. Fortress and Vulcans were considered, but the former was deemed inappropriate for a city which once could not defend itself against a small but resolute band of Indians, and Vulcans connotes not so much the noble Roman god of fire but the resurrection of worn automobile tires.

So it was the Maulers, city image be damned, and left now are only minor details—players, a playing site, a logo and team colors.

"Maybe a fist," suggests Beano Cook—a DeBartolo vice president and veteran thinker in such matters—"for a logo." The colors he deems as obvious as, well, a punch in the face: "Black and blue."

Random sampling of early reaction to the name seemed to indicate a 99-1 ratio, against. The people at the Chamber of Commerce are probably still strangling, but the Maulers will be heralded in every saloon where someone occasionally spits on the floor. Hereabouts, a guarantor of ultimate public acceptance, as it were.

After all, recent history clearly shows us willing to suffer a hockey team called the Penguins in honor of a bird that wears a perpetual look of confusion.

"Paul Martha tells me the intelligence of the penguin is underrated," Cook argues.

"My kids came home from the zoo the other day and said all the penguins were herded over in the corner of their enclosure, staring up at nothing," he is told.

"That's what the hockey team did all winter," says Cook, always quick to recognize a straight man.

In any case, the choice lifts one Marty Blake from an historical hook. In 1970, new to the city as general manager of a Pittsburgh professional basketball team, Blake conducted a contest to select a team nickname.

From the entries, he chose Pioneers, unfortunately then in use by Point Park College, which threatened to call its lawyer. Blake immediately retreated, only to have the lady who'd won the contest and its $500 first prize for suggesting Pioneers, threaten with her lawyer.

Faced with the need of coming up with another $500, Blake spent days searching for a name overlooked by any of the contestants. He struck on Condors. Ironically enough, a South American scavenger, rapidly becoming extinct because it could only lay one egg every two years. Which is precisely what the Condors did here before becoming defunct.

Undoubtedly, the name Maulers will also have its detractors and some unquestionably would've preferred a derivative other than the verb maul. Possibly whip, bang, buff, pound, abuse, maltreat or manhandle would've been better. Obviously, there was a certain distaste attached to molest.

But there are names far worse than the one which caught Ed DeBartolo's fancy—the NFL Dolphins, for one. Miami has a penchant for the ill-chosen nickname. Its World Football League entry was known as The Screaming Eagles.

Those of you who find Maulers unsatisfactory might take consolation in this: In the chicken-ranching area of New Jersey, the athletic teams of Union High School are known as The Poultry Clan.

Go, ah, Maulers.

As it turned out, the Maulers were ill-named, spectacularly unable to manage much mistreatment of their USFL opponents. They were colorful—their first coach got fired during a team crisis for refusing to meet with the owner—but on the field, they were merely mediocre. Their name failed to inspire ferocious accomplishments, unlike a fearsome Penn State defensive tackle of the late 1960s named Steve Smear. They did have a coach name Herring. Haering, actually.

Gone after one zany season, the Maulers are best-remembered for their fans' accuracy in throwing ice-balls at onetime Steeler quarterback Cliff Stoudt when he returned to Three Rivers Stadium in the livery of the Birmingham Stallions, and for their general ineffectiveness. The latter was manifested last year when, after it was widely-ballyhooed, the Maulers' planned reunion was canceled.

The Lonesome Death of Kathleen Conroy: Was Justice Denied?

TWELVE MEN good and true...

She turned into a lush, no question. And a tramp, maybe—although the cops and her few friends on the street insisted not. In any case, she abandoned her five kids for booze and vamping around a jukebox and singing softly to herself. She was variously regarded by some people who knew her as "slightly touched...a shell...harmless...childlike."

And she was white; the guy she lived with was black.

That ate at them, the prosecutor figures. That and the boozing, and swishing back and forth in front of a juke. And shacking up in the Hill.

So last week a jury—seven women and five men, of whom 11 were white—exchanged Kathleen Conroy's life for about five years of a man's time.

Early in their deliberations, the jurors had voted, 7 to 5, for first-degree murder. Later, they changed their minds. Some of them told prosecutor Chris Conrad that they hadn't approved of her lifestyle.

"It's often difficult for them to keep moral judgments out of their deliberations," Conrad says.

In fact, at the end of it, Kathleen Conroy's life wasn't much. Eight or nine years ago, though, she was a suburban housewife no different than most, except prettier, even after the booze had worn gullies under her eyes, a friend says. "Even then, you could always tell she'd been real pretty once."

And she was breezy and bright. A doting mother, it's said. Car pools. Clean, wash, cook. Occasional weekend night on the town. Nice buzz on three frosted daiquiris. Giggly. No more.

Mostly, she just took care of a family and carted her kid swimmers around to the different pools. She was kind of fierce about the meets, and was called a "Go, Johnny, go!" type.

Then, just before the Christmas of 1976, her life began unraveling.

An uncle she loved died. "He was sort of the cornerstone of our whole family," a niece says. He was the kind who bounced kids on his knees and always had an ice-cream cone handy.

Not long after the uncle died, a favorite nephew going to law school in New Mexico was murdered. Kathleen Conroy had often taken care of him. They were close.

Her marriage failed about then. She and her husband separated. She took the kids to Florida, couldn't find work and came back home. "She couldn't support the kids," says the niece, "and her husband got custody."

"The drinking started around then," says another relative.

One day, Kathleen Conroy just curled up in a quart of Jack Daniels and pretty much forgot about everything but singing to herself.

Last October, on a bitterly cold night and singing to herself, she scattered her clothes all around abandoned Fifth Avenue High School, where she'd gone with 20-year-old Gary Georgia to have sex, at her invitation, he said.

They argued, he tossed her off a fourth-floor corridor and she fell 40 feet to a marble floor. The fall could've killed her, the coroner said, but the point was moot. Either the bones Georgia snapped in her throat or the stick that tore through the wall in her vagina and caused fatal internal bleeding would've accomplished as much.

Georgia was tried by a jury of his peers, and the maximum he will draw for voluntary manslaughter is 5 to 10 years. He laughed, so a guard said afterward, all the way back to his cell.

Gary Georgia is 6-foot-4 and weighs 210 pounds. "Make an excellent tight end," a cop says. Kathleen Conroy was 5-foot-1, and weighed 100 pounds.

"The strangest and most surprising verdict I've ever had," Conrad was saying the other afternoon, hours before leaving on a vacation he needs now more than he did a week ago. "It was opposite to what the law would indicate. Voluntary manslaughter in any circumstance relative to this one would be a killing done in rage. It requires that rage to have had serious provocation by the victim."

Kathleen Conroy had been beyond rage for a long time. Death and lost kids and the DTs in a half-dozen drunk tanks and rehab centers had burned it out of her. It had left her singing to herself and swaying gently in front of jukeboxes.

"She was a shell, like a child, by then," says a niece, Rebecca Conroy. "But she was harmless. That's what's so sad. She wouldn't have even known she was in a dangerous situation."

John Harris, the man she lived with, tried to keep her out of harm's way.

"He washed her, bathed her; by all indications, there was a real relationship there," says Common Pleas Judge James R. McGregor, who heard the case and won't forget it for a while. He won't forget a flaw in the law that will let Gary Georgia walk in maybe 48 months.

"I just wish this jury had had a rape-by-instrument law to consider," McGregor sighs.

It didn't. There isn't one in Pennsylvania criminal law. But the jury that didn't like Kathleen Conroy's lifestyle didn't buy rape, either.

"Obviously that was our theory about the case, that the sexual act was not consental," says Chris Conrad. "She was torn very badly inside, bitten badly on the chest."

"One of the most solid cases to come through this Courtroom in a long time," he muses.

Not solid enough, though.

"I just can't believe it," Rebecca Conroy says. "We didn't want vengeance, just some kind of justice.

"You can't depend on the system."

No.

The night she was killed, Kathleen Conroy was feeding quarters into a jukebox and then swaying in front of it to the melody of a song called "Happy Birthday to Me."

Her death—perhaps unmatched in the county since in terms of brutality—provided an object lesson that changed the life of a Munhall woman far younger than Conroy.

Arrested for public intoxication and loitering, the Munhall woman was "sentenced" by Allegheny County Common Pleas Court Judge Gerard Bigley to sit through Gary Georgia's trial.

What she heard, it was reported, brought about a major change in her lifestyle.

After laughing at his sentence, Gary Georgia did his time.

It's time Virginia learns the truth about Christmas

THEY LIED TO YOU, VIRGINIA. There isn't any Santa Claus.

If there was, then there would be no need for Christmas shopping. And I would not be walking around in this manner today, as though small predators had been lunching on my insteps.

Ah, yes, we went Christmas shopping over the weekend, an exercise in anguish comparable only to having an appendage caught in the wringer. On Saturday morning, I was 46 and reasonably vigorous; Sunday evening, the numerals were reversed, I was but one more toy store away from shipment to the nearest home for the infirm, and my creditors had been served notice that their alternative to patience is Acme Collection Agency.

"Why are you walking that way?" the lady asked early Saturday afternoon.

"Because I'm trying to impress you with my Charlie Chaplin imitation," I snapped, a bone spur in my right foot making a grating noise with every step.

There are probably greater strains placed on marital bliss than Christmas shopping, but aside from sexual dysfunction or having a mother-in-law move in on a permanent basis, I can think of none.

Once, in the interest of shortening the agony, we separated and agreed to meet in the center of the mall. The lady missed the appointed moment by a scant 25 minutes.

"Where the hell were you?"

"Standing in a damn line for an hour!"

Like that.

By late afternoon, the eyes begin to glaze. The feet are sore to a degree that would alarm Dr. Scholl. Sheer fatigue has exhausted the ability to quarrel. And I have quit slamming my armload of packages into the solar plexuses of overly-aggressive old women. Desperation has brought us unity.

"Fighting Glogons," the lady says firmly, steering me to the nearest toy outlet.

"Fighting Glogons?"

They turn out to be molded plastic figures of prehistoric heroes: the Hill St. Blues of the Pleistocene Age. They come with various accouterments. Do we want mounted Glogons? The ones which throw spears or the ones with the stone clubs? In bilious green or blood rust?

Another kid wants a weapons system. In black or green? With the battle tank or without? Motorized? Whatever happened to cap guns, I ask the lady and go outside to flop down on a bench and smoke my 63rd Pall Mall of the day. Another father drops down beside me.

"Lord God Almighty," he sighs.

"Indeed," I respond.

We compare notes. If our figures are correct, he will be in debt four months longer than I will be, which is to say until March of 1987. I have already spent $4.75 in quarters to stuff presents in lockers at the other end of the building. He has long since run out of change, and periodically drags a load of stuff out to his car, which he says is parked just this side of Akron. He is almost done. I am keeping track on 3x5 index cards, one for each kid, and a conservative estimate indicates I will finish shopping just as the light goes out in Rudolph's nose.

"Good luck," he says, staggering off. A matron makes an abrupt turn no Porsche could negotiate, rams into him, glowers and says, "Watch where the hell you're going."

"Merry Christmas," he says, hobbling away.

Glogons in hand, the lady returns, but with bad news. We have blundered badly, a gift purchased at one store is spied on sale at another at considerable savings. We attempt to return the gizmo to a clerk who trained for her position at Dachau.

"Receipt!"

"It's here somewhere," I plead, sorting through a hundred pieces of paper in disparate sizes and shapes while a herd paws the floor behind me, grumbling ominously.

"C'mon, buddy."

"Hey, Mac, come back when you find it."

"Receipt!" the Dragon Lady commands.

I tear a pocket loose from its mooring and wave the damn piece of paper triumphantly.

"Wrong department," sneers the clerk. "Next!"

In time, my tears dry, and the search presses on, the lady indefatigable as she sorts through thermal underwear for an offspring currently living in the sub-tropics.

"Whyinhell does he want thermal underwear?"

"I don't know," she says, infuriatingly unflappable. "Shall we get the bottoms too?"

"By all means. And a fur hat."

The day wears on, my foot throbbing and one thigh frozen where a little kid had raced into me, thrust his ice-cream cone against my leg, pivoted using it for leverage, and roared away, knocking an old lady off the top step of the escalator.

"Billeee," screamed a frantic mother in pursuit.

Darkness falls and we're still at it, credit cards ravaged, stumbling, redeyed, frothing at the mouth. The lady makes a final remark on the final 3x5 card. I am fantasizing wildly about a double-martini. The lady pauses and says, "What shall we get my mother?"

I almost tell her.

The lady described above and I have not gone Christmas shopping together in more than a decade and the kid who wanted the Fighting Glogons recently graduated from high school. Before he did, the Bright-Eyed Girl was pressed into service and she still fondly recalls the endless but ultimately successful search for the Roton Assault Vehicle.

Some years, I went shopping for as many as 13 kids. Biological kids. Step-kids. Adopted kids. Cambodian kids. Kids of all sizes, shapes, colors, religions,, nationalities, and haircuts. In stores side-by-side, I once bought the aforementioned Glogons and a lace teddy for a teenager. In the above column, like Shakespeare's lady, I doth protest too much.

All the kids have attained their majority and some are multiplying. A new love promises to add a dozen and a half kids and grand-kids to my list.

A rough estimate of my 1994 list is, believe it or not, 32. I started shopping in February.

Joe Gilliam shows there isn't an ounce of quit in him

FOR A LONG TIME, HE WAS A JUNKIE. Nobody was ever in deeper. A Moped could've made a U-turn in his nose.

He snorted a thousand Mexican heroin fantasies, lived the great white pipe dream and fell from grace like a rock. He lied and stole and jived everyone who was ever precious to him.

In time, dope cost him every last thing he had. His wife. A daughter who, when he talked about her, his eyes would turn moist. His pride, and once he had a flat ton of it. His health. And finally the dignity that always burned in his eyes. The last shreds of it got lost when a cop found him hunkering in his mother's clothes closet and when a couple of street punks in Baltimore smashed in the windows of a parked car and dragged him across the shards of glass and beat him bloody with pick handles because a coke deal had gone wrong.

But, Lord, does he have moxie.

That's what this column is about. The moxie of an unsinkable man. His indomitability. Beat Joey Gilliam flatter than a shadow and sooner or later, he will lurch back onto his feet. And reach for a football.

But this isn't about football. Compulsion, maybe. A strange sort of courage that shines bright enough to read by. But not football. Just a guy who keeps on truckin', no matter what.

Joe Gilliam got fired again the other day by a dust rag of a football team, the Washington Federals of the United States Football League. He's been booted by better.

Even Joey must've had to laugh at the reason. A lot of Federal customers are black. A month ago, the team acquired a high-priced but unproven young quarterback named Reggie Collier, who is also black. So's Joe Gilliam. Old and forgotten black.

"I'm not discouraged," he told the Associated Press. "I knew what was happening. I'll catch on with another team. Somebody had to go."

So Jefferson Street Joe Gilliam went, but not with finality.

The Federals are about the 12th team to cut him adrift since he rose like a star with the Steelers in 1974 and burned to a cinder in 24 months. The New Orleans Saints tried to redeem him a couple of times, but he would throw the ball wonderfully in practice, then nod off in a heroin haze during meetings.

There were three or four semipro teams. He'd lift them by the nape to whatever heights were attainable, the smack would use him up, he'd move on. The fast gun with the big habit.

In Baltimore, he threw the ball like Johnny Unitas and did dope. In Houston, he finally got off the junk and burned up the Texas League and the no-names went for his knees and his head.

"I'm the only guy in the league anyone's ever heard of," he explained. "But it's OK. I've got to get used to the pass rush."

In the last two years, a couple of National Football League teams, Dallas and Detroit, liked him, but old women don't fear snakes the way the NFL fears dope. "Some club's going to give me a break," he would always insist when I'd run across him.

Finally the desperate USFL clubs tried him out. Denver. Los Angeles. Finally, Washington. He played a half-dozen games for the pathetic Federals last spring on an ankle that looked like an eggplant and threw his high, hard one the way he had here. But Reggie Collier is the bright future and Joe Gilliam just the regrettable past.

Still, there isn't an ounce of quit in him. Never has been. In 1972, he was that rarest of novelties, a black pro quarterback. A national magazine was so enamored of the idea that they hired me to write a story called The Trials of a Black Rookie Quarterback.

The day I met him, he said, "If they give me a chance, I'll put Bradshaw on the bench. I can do it, man. I really can do it."

I remember lifting his arm up and asking, "What color is this?"

"Yeah...I know," he'd smiled. "But I can do it."

We used to get together late at night at the training camp snack bar, where he'd drink two or three thick milkshakes and chain-smoke. "Only thing I can keep on my stomach, milkshakes and Kools," he'd say. "If they just give me a chance, I can make it."

One night his dad, a college coach, told me that when Joe Jr. was six, he'd sleep propped up in the doorway to his parents' bedroom so that Joe Sr. would have to wake him up every morning when he was leaving for practice.

"He wouldn't let me go without him; even then, football was everything he wanted," Joe's father said.

And Joe Gilliam, a kid with legs that looked like a couple of clarinets but a .357 arm, could throw it. As well as Terry Bradshaw, maybe better. I wrote a line so often about him "throwing coppery streaks across the sky," that a few friends still kid me about it.

The last time I saw him was a few years ago in a New Orleans hotel during Super Bowl week. He was playing for the Dixie Stars and starting in a national minor-league all-star game the next day.

"Come by to see Coach Noll," he said softly that day in a voice that always hinted of magnolias and gentility and deep-south twilight. "Wanted to thank him for all that he taught me."

No, he said, he wasn't going to quit. "Minor-league ball keeps my hand in. One of these days, Jefferson Street Joe Gilliam will be back."

Soon, he will be, again. Somewhere. Somehow.

The dope got him, again. No matter how far he gets from it,
smack calls him home with a siren song that, sooner or later, he can't

quite resist. The last time, he held it at bay for several years.

When he could no longer dance loose from the pass rush, and when the heavy-calibre arm finally went the way of all flesh, he coached with Joe Sr. at Tennessee State and became a motivational speaker. Got up there with flashing eyes and brimstone voice and told kids about the evils of dope. I heard him once and he reminded me some of Jimmy Swaggart. People would've stood in the rain to listen to him speak. But a while back came the inevitable wire service story. Joey Gilliam had been busted for, what, the zillionth time on a dope charge.

The pity of it is, of course, the abandoned potential on the football field, and off. Birds would leave their nest if he called...he had that much charm.

As for football, he could throw tracer bullets and the year the Steelers claimed their first Super Bowl trophy, he put Terry Bradshaw on the bench for a while. But a dealer could always smell Joey Gilliam from a dozen blocks away. And, in time, one invariably located him. They probably always will. Not that the moxie is gone, you understand. He is no less resilient in his 40s than he was in his 20s. Another comeback? Sure. But everyone's quit counting.

Emergency room prescription is compassion and care

AT 2:30 A.M. TUESDAY, a mean wind is whispering across the dark parking lot behind the emergency entrance to Forbes Regional Health Center in Monroeville. It mutes soft cries.

"Few more feet," the man says to the 15-year old, who has long been a trooper on such visits. Little finger almost cut off in an accident when she was little. Broken leg as a toddler. Complex oral surgery just a while back.

"OK," she says stoically, walking bent over against the pain.

Inside the entrance, pretty, red-haired nurse Judy Benzel takes one quick look at Kari Moon's face, says, "c'mon, honey," and has the girl in a wheelchair in 10 seconds flat and on the way to a treatment room.

"We need some information, sir," says Joan Sontheimer, the emergency room receptionist. Fatigue has rubbed dark smudges under her eyes, but she briskly threads a form into an electric typewriter and looks up. Something she sees in the man's face makes her hesitate.

He's been in emergency rooms many times before. Some of them were butcher shops. He's not very interested in forms right now.

"No," assures Joan Sontheimer, who has been at the job long enough to read minds. "She's being taken care of right now. They won't wait."

The information is recorded and he is sent back to the treatment room where the doctor on the overnight shift, Bill Edwards, has already made a preliminary examination and done some tests.

There is severe abdominal pain, some vague symptoms which suggest an early appendicitis. He stares into space for a long moment. The diagnosis is not easy. He makes a telephone call upstairs to Dr. Tim Hielman.

The man sits on a chair beside the bed in the treatment room and does what can be done in such moments. Rubs her back, listens to the small whimperings, and feels totally helpless.

Forbes Regional is quiet this night. The heating system kicks in and hums its urgent message; voices are magnified, carrying harshly down long hallways. In a nearby waiting room, the Cable News Network drones on. Taking a smoke break, he hears two children have died in a Chicago fire and shivers. There are things far worse than uncertainty.

Jim Bryan, an unemployed construction worker, peels off a sheepskin jacket and Navy watch cap, and fires up the first of many Camels he'll smoke during the night. He is a salt-of-the-earth workingman. Thickset; big, tattooed forearms, beat-up hands. Out of work now, he frets over it, but saves his real concern for "those poor guys losing their houses, their families falling apart, people with not enough to eat. Things could be worse for me."

His father has just come in with abdominal bleeding. Worry hovers in Bryan's eyes. His Dad is 80 years old. Over the weekend, he'd gone down to the Wilmerding American Legion for a few beers.

"He says, 'It was the Stroh's,'" Bryan laughs. "Says, 'If I'd been drinking Iron City, I wouldn't be here!'"

Time inches by, one minute at a time. Back in treatment room 1, Hielman, down from pediatrics, is reassuring as his fingers probe the girl's abdomen. He looks as young as his patient, speaks gently.

"I know this hurts," he says. "But it'll be over soon."

In the hallway moments later, while Kari finally begins to doze, he says maybe it's appendicitis, maybe it's not. He and Edwards talk, decide on consultation. "There's another doctor...we call him The Professor," Edwards explains with a smile. "I'd like him to see her. Why don't you get some coffee and we'll call you."

The man and Jim Bryan talk quietly for what seems hours, CNN giving way to a show on psoriasis. Bonds grow quickly in these places. They agree that "when we were kids, people seemed closer to each other somehow." Both long for that time as they eat Camels and machine coffee, and fidget.

As they settle the world's problems, the night wears on and other patients check into Forbes Regional emergency. A man with a badly lacerated leg. A baby with a raging fever. An 80-year old woman with chest pains. A middle-aged female victim of an automobile accident who will later die. The treatment is quick and caring.

"A slow night for us, though," sighs Judy Benzel.

A guy feels the need to say thanks. To say that Swiss watches seem no more efficient than this place. To wonder if maybe emergency rooms get a bad rap.

"A lot of it depends on what is happening with you when you're there," Judy Benzel says. "Some places probably are bad. Here, we try hard not to be."

Even the kid mopping the hall by the reception area seems professional, his mop catching each corner.

The Professor arrives and his examination is lengthy and unhurried. He decides he will admit Kari Moon for observation.

A tear rolls down her cheek. She'd wanted to go to school. A boy friend must be called.

"Can I use the telephone?"

"Nope, I'll call him."

"Tell Mom to bring me pajamas and a hair brush and some makeup and a radio."

As the man goes to the telephone, dawn has broken cleanly over the horizon on a cold, clear morning. Judy Benzel pulls on her coat, Joan Sontheimer straightens her desk, Jim Bryan tugs on the watch cap and sticks out a hard hand, Drs. Heilman and Edwards yawn and anticipate needed sleep.

"Thanks," says the man, who owes them all.

The guard changes and the Forbes Regional emergency room hums on, without missing a beat.

I once took a kid into an emergency room and was told later by a frustrated doctor, "Don't bring him back unless there is a bone sticking through his skin."

On the above occasion, the patient was well-mannered and her symptoms disappeared quickly. Conversely, my memories of that night have lingered, even though Kari Ann Domaneck (nee' Moon) has long since visited a hospital emergency room with her own daughter.

I guess my feelings have to do with vulnerability. With the nauseating awareness that, in such a place, a father can no longer fool himself that he is truly his child's protector.

I don't know what lawyers or hod-carriers or insurance salesmen do in such straits; writers take surreptitious notes and later try to make sense of the experience by writing about it.

Then, some long time later, they foist their musings off on unsuspecting readers under the guise that they have almost certainly shared a similar experience.

It's a slow day in the city - even Purgatory is closed

It is the slowest news day of the year, Dec. 26. Even City Council is benevolently silent. A night-shift reporter rubs fatigue from his eyes, tugs on his jacket and leaves. Only the hum of the heating system disturbs the late-morning silence in the office. A guy with a column to write sips coffee, looks out a window at the gray void, and his imagination shoots blanks. It is mean cold, that's a thought. It is a lonely sort of a day, that's an idea, too. He gets his coat.

Hamp—"jes' Hamp"—shuffles through the early afternoon and up Penn Avenue past Horne's, toward the Greyhound station. He leans into the cutting wind, the muscles in his stomach involuntarily tightening when it finds its way through the dingy, black greatcoat.

"Cold muthah," he cackles in an ageless voice.

Hamp doesn't like the day after Christmas, with its emptiness, its holiday hangover, its gray solitude.

"Too quiet," he explains. "Nobody out. Everybody home."

He pulls his head down into the coat, so that the flaring collar hides all but the tight gray-black cap of hair.

"Purgatory closed," he says accusingly.

Purgatory is a joint over on Liberty. You can get a glass of cheap muscatel there that sets your belly on fire for 30 seconds and while you're drinking it, you can watch girls take their clothes off. Hamp prefers the wine. As he prefers his privacy. "Jes' Hamp," he repeats, for emphasis.

Crystal snowflakes drift down through sunshine that lacks warmth, reflecting light like tiny prisms. Plodding along, Hamp gingerly fingers his right ear, testing it as though it had become too brittle for touch. Apparently it hasn't and he rolls the lobe between his fingertips, the way you might test a particularly fine piece of fabric. Satisfied, he rubs the ear as briskly as he would a large, furry dog.

The other ear is tended to. Nothing much can be done about the nose, although Hamp tentatively rubs it back and forth a few times on a coat sleeve. Hands shuffled briskly, he stamps his feet a few times and takes up the journey.

When the wind blows, the chill-factor dips to well below zero. Faces grow stiff and even talking becomes difficult.

"Where you sleeping tonight?" a guy asks.

"Slept today...parking garage," Hamp says, stopping again to stamp some blood back into his feet. There is disgust in the weary voice: Don't you know nothin', boy? "Walk tonight."

Hamp plods on toward the bus station to defrost. A horn toots a couple of times, blown by a man with one of the most-recognizable faces in the city. Franco Harris smiles and waves. His grin asks the obvious—what the hell are you doing walking around town?—and the car turns out of sight.

67

It is mostly a day for shoppers, scurrying early for transportation to the comfort of home.

"Best day of the year for bargains," confides a stout, smiling woman with her arms loaded. "I don't mind the weather. Wouldn't miss this for anything."

The guy hurries to keep the blood circulating as the sun recedes behind fat plum-colored clouds. Hamp's shuffle doesn't slow as the streets seem to empty with even the first hint of afternoon's demise.

Faces are hidden by scarves or obscured in billowing, white breaths. A man with crimson cheeks hugs the buildings against the icy gusts, mumbling to himself, as he passes going the other direction.

"Have to do it," he says. And, more secure with the thought, says it again as he disappears around a corner. Hamp shakes his head. "Man's touched," he says.

A teen-age daughter holds her blind father's elbow firmly and leads him across a street made treacherous by sheets of dirty, dark ice. His cane licks at the street, making cricket sounds. A PAT bus roars down on them, as they inch their way to the far sidewalk, passers-by watching and taking quick breaths in anticipation. Of what? Disaster? The vulnerable reaching safety? They do, and are immediately forgotten.

A departing sun leaves the day so clear and crisp that the blare of a car horn can be heard a mile. Hamp passes a couple of men huddled deep in a doorway. One of them says something unintelligible. He pays no attention. The bus station, squatty and pale, is just a block away. His step quickens a bit.

"Coffee be good," he says, looking straight ahead, head bowed.

"Real good," agrees a guy with an expense account. "Bet a few glasses of wine might go down pretty easy, too."

At the corner, they stop. Hamp nods and slips into the warmth of the Greyhound station, while the guy turns back down Liberty Avenue toward the office.

Like Hamp, one day Purgatory just disappeared, leaving Downtown without a real burnout bar where you could watch slatternly women take off their clothes and drink Muscatel that could etch glass.

The winos remain, of course. On bitter nights, they fight the rats for space on the big heating grates of the Downtown office buildings. Some sleep on flattened cardboards in Point State Park until the cops roust them. Mostly, they walk and suck on the Ripple or Thunderbird, with its illusion of warmth.

Hardly ever do their wornout bodies clutter the streets or our eyes. A social worker once told me, "They die in small increments."

Nobody ever seems to know their names. "Jes' Hamp." They are, in fact, interchangeable. Once in a while, a politician tries to pass legislation to keep them from bothering decent people. Winos is too harsh a description these politically-correct days. Now we call them panhandlers.

The Best of Phil Musick

Some memories diminish the joy of his reincarnation

IN AN EARLIER INCARNATION, I was a sportswriter, which is a lingering form of adolescence.

Some few months ago, though, I finally made the transition into the real world, and now when I return to the family hearth for a night, the kids do not run around the next morning confiding to the neighbors that their mother is sleeping with a stranger.

In truth, I hadn't missed the world of sweaty amusements even a twit. Not until this week, when the Steelers began girding themselves to beard the Raiders, formerly of Oakland, in their new habitat in Los Angeles. Then, the old calling fairly grabbed me by the neck.

Once more, the Steelers and the Raiders will do battle unto death in the National Football League playoffs and, alas, I will be there in spirit only. Stuck in front of the tube with all those memories of great games and grand stories and delightful rogues far too numerous for any one columnist to accommodate.

Ah, there was the spice of the sportswriting life. The Steelers and the Raiders. Luke and Darth. Art Rooney's cigar and wonderful benevolence and Oakland Al Davis' mirror sunglasses and marvelous deceit. The Immaculate Reception and the Criminal Element. And the two toughest, funniest, feistiest, proudest teams in professional football.

They didn't "meet" or "play", those two. They collided in great, colorful, billowing clouds of greenstick fractures and breath-catching games and attendant skullduggery.

Has there ever been a rivalry so rich in lore and intrigue and the purer forms of mean-spirited deception? Probably not. The era of honorable enemies has departed the NFL, lost to television ratings and bitter labor relations and institutionalized parity. But before it did, it was housed in the humor and mystery and intensity which attended each meeting of the Steelers and the Raiders.

It began, this love-hate business, innocently enough over a film exchange in 1972. The Raiders swore they shipped Chuck Noll the required two scouting films. Only one arrived.

"It's out of focus," announced the tight-lipped Noll, who found small humor in the incident and arranged for Oakland to practice locally not at Three Rivers Stadium, but at Monument Hill field. When the Raiders alighted from their buses, they sank to their knees. The field was a bog.

When a Raider player was beaten by police the night before the game and Franco Harris' Immaculate Reception shockingly thrust favored Oakland out of the playoffs, a fuse was lit that still burns. Yesterday, the Raiders wouldn't even let Press sportswriter Ron Cook into the club offices.

"The Immaculate Reception was the start of the NFL conspiracy against the

Raiders," swears former Oakland defensive back Willie Brown to this day.

Thereafter, no Steeler-Raider confrontation ever lacked fiery controversy. Steeler center Ray Mansfield bent over to snap for an extra-point attempt in Oakland in 1973 and found the ball was partially deflated. "What the hell?" he protested. The next ball thrown in from the sidelines was inscribed with an obscene and physiologically impossible suggestion.

The following years produced no fewer high jinks.

When Oakland offensive linemen were accused of using a foreign substance on the backs of their jerseys to prevent Steeler defensive linemen from getting a hand-hold, Raider guard George Buehler protested to Steeler linebacker Andy Russell: "Honest, Andy, I'm 100 percent American. It wasn't a foreign substance. It was Vaseline."

The night before a 1975 playoff game here, a tarp covering the field during an early-morning ice storm came unmoored at the edges and left the sidelines treacherous during the game. The Steelers announced it had torn. Oakland Al Davis, forced to watch fleet receiver Cliff Branch rendered useless by the frozen turf, swore, "it was purposely slashed." Questioned about it, Danny Rooney still smiles.

Sadly, the next year the antagonists became truly bitter.

Noll fingered Raider defensive backs George Atkinson and Jack Tatum as part of the league's "criminal element." And when the Steelers lost a playoff game to Oakland that year without the injured Franco Harris and Rocky Bleier, Oakland Al burned furiously at the suggestion their absence was a major factor. Of Oakland's victory over the Steelers in the next season's opener, Davis cried, "Our greatest win!"

Still, no Raider victory could ever quite remove the sting of the 1974 loss that sent the Steelers on to their first Super Bowl trophy. The memory of that one lingers. Sitting on the team bus in the parking lot of Oakland-Alameda County Stadium after the Steelers had won and watching a beaten Davis trudge to his Continental, pain evident in each step. And Terry Hanratty yanking open a window and pouring laughing invective down upon the bowed head. And then smiling, "Al's not so bad, but nothing could ever be as sweet as this is."

Not in the memory of an ex-sportswriter, anyway.

The steady hum of the passing years blurs even the dramatic moments, turns them up the backwaters of the memory so far they're irretrievably lost. Happens even to aging, one-time sportswriters, who saw most of what there was to see amongst the sweaty arts for two decades. And has forgotten a lot of it.

A few memories have negotiated that tricky passage we call time. Secretariat...Big Red...fleeing through the homestretch in the 1973 Belmont Stakes. A floating, burnished crimson shadow who would win by 30 some lengths and whose great heart made even the hard-

ened rail birds weep. A couple of Roberto Clemente throws from the deep shadows of the right-field corner that made the breath catch in the throat. The sweep and majesty of Lemieux. Some Super Bowls. A prize fight or three. Michael and Magic, any old time. And those Black Magic antagonists, the Steelers and the Raiders, in their 60-minute wars.

If I live to be a thousand, I will not forget the look of pure glee on Terry Hanratty's face or the triumph in his voice the afternoon he mocked a defeated Al Davis. It was as much fun as sex.

Nah, but you get the idea.

The lady won the love of all but the one who counted

ONCE, SHE WAS a raging sex queen, and the symbol of detente between two superpowers, and an international star, and about the cutest little trick around.

Only John F. Kennedy's libido was ever under more scrutiny than hers but if she couldn't quite hack it as a lover, over the years she more than made up for it. Or a couple of generations of kids and no small number of adults thought so. Now, sadly, she's dying.

Ling-Ling, the lady panda, has a critical kidney ailment and is near death at the Washington, D.C., National Zoo, interested not in the bamboo she loved to munch or even old Hsing-Hsing, the failed Lothario with whom she's kept company and pursued ardently since 1972.

"It's a day-to-day thing," says a zoo veterinarian, "not something we can accurately predict."

That's Ling-Ling, unpredictable to the end. Been that way since the People's Republic of China sent her and Hsing-Hsing—pronounced Shing-Shing—West during the time of ping-pong diplomacy.

Richard Nixon and Chairman Mao had been staring at one another unblinkingly for years before the pandas helped bring about the great thaw between the PRC and the U.S.

Not that it was any great trick for pandas to charm cold-war politicians as easily as they do the rest of us. Outsized cousins of raccoons, pandas are about as lovable as anything in nature. Black and white, cuddly for all their size. Among the most playful of creatures. They're terrific, pandas are. Can't fool a kid.

Maybe the Reds were still the same dirty, inscrutable bunch we'd fought in Korea, we all thought in those days, but how bad could old Mao really be if he could give us a cute little Ling-Ling and the chance to one day have zoos full of marvelous pandas?

Alas, it never happened. Each spring, a hopeful nation would watch expectantly, sure that Hsing-Hsing would finally take the hint. And each fall, the editorial writers would hunch over their typewriters to sigh once more over the failure of panda romance.

Hey, not that Ling-Ling wasn't willing to bat an eye or two for the cause, you understand. When she was younger, she'd roll over on her back and cover her eyes coyly with one paw, and give him the old come-on. But Hsing-Hsing, disgustingly healthy to this day, proved a clod. About the only suggestive move he ever displayed was to try to stand on his head for her when he was still pretty much of a cub and not yet up to a mature relationship.

For a year or so, they occupied separate sleeping quarters. "Till they're ready" we were told. As it turned out, seducing Hsing-Hsing took longer than the Seven Years War.

In season twice a year, Ling-Ling would give him her slinkiest look and ask, "Your place or mine, big boy?" And Hsing-Hsing would just chew up another bale of bamboo and wander off. Probably to watch Monday Night Football.

"She would just sit and cry for him," a vet once explained.

Pandas, it seems, would provide a ton of research for Masters and Johnson. A few years ago, another couple had their difficulties in the London Zoo, Lan-Lan and An-An. Lan-Lan was a vixen, but remained barren to her death. An-An had a mad passion for his trainer.

Ling-Ling was a bit more persistent than Lan-Lan, though, and never quit fanning the torch for Hsing-Hsing.

"Maybe she should blow in his ear," a zoo official once said in disgust.

It may have come to that this spring. In any case, after a decade of headaches, Hsing-Hsing's fancy finally turned from bamboo and Ling-Ling conceived. You could almost hear the editorialists' sigh of relief. Thousands of people volunteered to baby-sit at the zoo. The first lady came around to pay her respects. Panda-lovers everywhere went out to buy the cigars.

Ironically, Ling-Ling delivered a male cub in late July, but it only lived three hours and the pregnancy is believed to have led to the kidney failure which is threatening her life.

Ling-Ling's death would be particularly untimely because a bamboo blight in the Chinese province of Sichuan threatens the survival of the thousand or so remaining pandas. The Chinese forestry ministry has already announced that no pandas will be sent abroad for at least two years.

That's a pity, because Ling-Ling's prognosis doesn't look too good. Probably all those cold, lonely nights.

Ling-Ling, alas, fled this vale of tears not long after this was written, but the pandas continue to be the National Zoo's most-compelling attraction. If memory serves, in the past decade a couple of pandas have conceived and borne healthy offspring, but the weak libido of the animals remains a concern. To zookeepers and zoo visitors, anyway.

Maybe it's something in the bamboo.

The situation is mindful of a remark made long ago about sex by an anonymous wit: "What one can do with ease, two mangle."

Finally, there is something deliciously ironic about a circumstance in which the favorite specie of the most populous nation in the world has great difficulty propagating.

Christmas story of caring seems to cry for an encore

HE REMEMBERS it as though it happened yesterday, enjoys it more than anything Dickens did on the subject. It's his all-time favorite Christmas story.

"It was a week before Christmas," he was musing after the deadline had been whipped for one more day. "I got a call at the paper from some guy, saying Harvey Thompson's house was on fire down in this little town I covered."

That it was, flames quickly consuming the small home to its cinder-block foundation. A few hours later, he was back in the office, "writing a tear-jerker."

Harvey had eight kids and had lost everything in the fire. A family of 10 was homeless, stone-broke and without hope, six days before Christmas. He milked the story to the last dripping adjective.

"Well, it was a hell of a story," he sniffs.

The public surely thought so. Contributions began to trickle into the paper for the poor Thompsons. A refrigerator. A few boxes of clothing and food. The offer of temporary housing.

"People were genuinely touched," he says, "so I went to the editor and suggested that maybe an editorial would be appropriate. You know...a family destitute during the holidays, badly in need of help, a time for giving. He said to write it and we made it the lead editorial the next day."

It has been often said that, whatever our other faults, no people are quite so generous as Americans.

"It was the damnedest thing I've ever been involved in...you had to be there," he says. "The whole thing began with that damn editorial. First people started calling, wanting to help. Then the stuff started piling up at the front door."

The next morning, reporters had to climb over a mountain of donations to get into the paper.

"All hell broke loose," he says. "Let's see...we got a car. Somebody donated the use of a house. We got six refrigerators. Five stoves. Fourteen beds. Maybe 50 boxes of clothing. And a lot of money.

"It just kept coming in."

The closer to Christmas Day it got, the deeper the public reached into its pockets for the less-fortunate.

"Old Harvey, he would come into the office about every 20 minutes to thank us," he remembers, some laughter perking in his voice.

The business community was no less charitable than were individuals who had been moved by the Thompsons' plight. The electricians and carpenters' unions donated their time and materials to put the new house in livable condition.

"A company donated the use of a couple of trucks to haul the stuff down to Harvey's new house," he says. "Another company put in all new windows and doors. The place was fixed up pretty nice."

On Christmas morning, the family was settled comfortably in its new home. All 10 were awash with presents. Turkey and trimmings had been sent along by a thoughtful grocer. And nobody could quite bring themselves to believe the rumors that had been circulating back to the paper.

"Oh, we heard that Harvey was carrying the stuff out the back door as fast as we were bringing it in the front door," he says, "but Harvey was such a nice, old guy...we didn't pay any attention to the talk."

After the holidays, the reporter and the man who owned the local radio station were asked to be in charge of a fund which had sprung up in the wake of the family's tragedy.

"There were several thousand dollars," he says, "and it became a headache for us to both have to OK every expenditure. Finally, we got together and said 'the hell with this', so we just drew every dollar out of the bank and gave him a check."

The paper wrote a final story after the holidays. Few communities would've been so unselfish, it said. A fine deed had been done. Prosperity snatched from the ashes. The whole town could be proud. And, by implication, the paper had also served its readers pretty well.

No story could've had a nicer ending, but nothing is deader than yesterday's news and the incident was quickly forgotten.

"The next Christmas, to the very damn day," he says, "I got another call from the same guy who'd called the year before.

"Harvey Thompson's house had burned down."

The story was true, down to the smallest detail. The reporter was Dave Ailes—then covering city hall for the Greensburg Tribune-Review; for the last 26 years the newspaper's sports editor. The name of the guy, who almost surely had torched his own house and made a mockery of sweet charity, was changed to protect the innocent and because his deceit would've been difficult to prove.

Ailes still loves to tell the story on himself, although until his death years afterward, the paper's editor, Tom Aikens, would turn the air purple with profanity at even the mention of it.

A digression. This book does not include a column on Aikens, although if there is a sequel to it, that will be the first entry.

Tom Aikens Sr. was the consummate newspaperman. He loved his wife and children, strong coffee, about any brand of beer you'd care to name, chain-smoking Kools and the Tribune-Review. Not necessarily in that order. Most years, he won the Pennsylvania Newspaper Publishers Association award for editorial writing. He died a relatively young man and it's probably not melodramatic to suggest that his love for, and commitment to, the newspaper had as much to do with his demise as anything else. He would've had it no other way. Once, when the necessity of mowing his lawn threatened to cut into his 12-14 hour days at the paper, Aikens immediately threatened to have his grass replaced with Astroturf. On another occasion, after two libel suits had been filed against the newspaper in the space of a few days, he put the following note on the newsroom bulletin board: "We've been sued for libel twice this week. What are the rest of you doing?"

I worked for him for three years. To bastardize the title of Robert Fulghum's best-seller, all I ever needed to know, I learned in front of Tom Aikens' desk.

Dad joins daughter in death so she wouldn't be alone

HIS LITTLE GIRL WAS DEAD. Beyond his reach. His help. His love.

Death must be the ultimate loneliness, he thought. The ultimate fear. He could not bear her facing it alone.

Perhaps no pain ever cuts quite as deeply as the cold agony a father can feel for a daughter. Their broken bodies can heal. Time blots the anguish of the deepest disappointment. Even the greatest failure of one moment can yield to success in another.

But when they are alone with their fear, and from their birth you have been their shield, that is a special hell. Sometimes it is not endurable.

It wasn't for Paul Hullihen.

When the doctor told him that his youngest daughter was dead, he sat down in a hospital waiting room, gathered himself fiercely, stared at the far wall, and understood only that in death, she would be afraid and alone. He made a decision. He would join her shortly.

He would will it to happen.

Less than 48 hours later, it did.

"He didn't say much when they told us Sherry had passed away," Belle Hullihen was saying yesterday afternoon from her home in Big Run, a little town near Punxsutawney. "He had such a bad look on his face. Such a bad color. He said, 'It should've been me. I'm old. She had so much ahead of her, so much to live for. It should've been me.'"

Sherry Young was killed 10 days ago when her car collided head-on with a truck. She was 28; her father's daughter. Her Dad was 71; a pretty tough guy. He'd landed at Normandy on D-Day and was on a troop ship in the Pacific when World War II ended. He'd worked a lifetime in a steel mill. But there is a limit to any strength.

"I've never seen a man in such agony," Belle Hullihen says quietly. She is a soft-spoken woman, keeps her own counsel: "A strong woman," says a friend. Maybe there is some small comfort in believing her husband chose his destiny. Of that, she has no doubt.

"He kept saying, 'The hurt just won't go away,'" she says.

The morning of Feb. 6, Sherry Young had stopped to have coffee with her mother. She was temporarily out of work and the hours dragged by. Her husband was working in Clarion.

"Sherry said she was lonesome, that she wished Russ was home, so she decided to drive over to see him," Belle Hullihen says. "On the way home...we don't know what happened. They think a ball-joint broke."

The next day, Paul Hullihen began saying that if he was with his daughter, she would not be afraid.

"I'm going with Sherry," he told his wife.

His family tried to comfort him. They said all the right things. Told him he was needed. Loved. The pain didn't recede.

"Paul, you still have three children...five beautiful grandchildren. We all need you."

Paul Hullihen was adamant. His wife and children would have each other. They were strong people. They would comfort one another. Sherry was alone.

"She needs me more," he insisted again and again. "I'm going with her."

The next night, another daughter, her husband and children came to stay at the Hullihen home.

"I'm going," Paul Hullihen told them. Scared, one of the kids tried to nudge his grandfather from his resolve with a joke.

"You're going where? To bed, Pa?"

"No, with Sherry. If not today, tomorrow."

He fell asleep in a chair at the kitchen table and his son-in-law later helped him to bed.

At 1 a.m., Hullihen awakened and said, "I want to talk," Belle Hullihen remembers, "but he just put an arm across me and fell back asleep."

At 3 a.m., Paul Hullihen stirred again, waking his wife.

"I've got a pain in my chest, Belle," he said.

"What do you want me to get you?" she asked.

"Oh, nothing."

An hour or so later, worried that a grandchild was crying, he went downstairs.

"I heard my daughter scream," Belle Hullihen says. "I knew."

Her husband was rushed to the hospital. He had suffered a fatal heart attack.

"He got what he wanted," his wife says, having buried her daughter and her husband one day apart. "The undertaker showed me the death certificate. He said, 'I never saw anything like this.'

"It read, 'Died of a broken heart, due to a family tragedy.'"

It is not always lovers who, in song and rhyme anyway, die of broken hearts. By all accounts, Paul Hullihen was, too, a victim of pain too mean and unrelenting to bear.

A Roman emperor once observed to his favorite advisor, "There are stranger things in this world than in all of your philosophies, Cicero."

In writing more than 1,500 of these columns, this was probably the strangest story I ran across. Doctors insist that often the determinant between life and death is a person's will. Perhaps that was the case here.

I'm not sure anything more can be legitimately said. Not by me, anyway.

What's more refreshing than a spring day in February?

SPRING SUNK ITS TEETH into winter's neck yesterday in the gloaming of a gentle, sunny afternoon uncommon to this meanest of months.

Oh, the death throes are some weeks off, but there was a rich feel to the day that strongly suggests we will soon thaw for good and be rid of this foul season.

The jogger felt that portent as he swung off the street and down onto the wharf that runs along the Mon to the Point. No bitter wind blowing up the Ohio into his bones. The sun warm on his face and throwing long shadows across the huge stone blocks under his feet.

On a distant bench in Point State Park, a man and a woman huddle together in the crowded silhouette that unmistakably signals love, or sincere lust. Their conversation is animated, their smiles knowing and the challenge in their eyes bespeaking intimacy. A preening song sparrow with clear squatter's rights to the bench sits on the top slat, a foot off the man's shoulder, resolute and combative. Sequins of sunlight dance on the river in front of the couple.

Of the city's three rivers, the Monongahela is the laziest. And, contrarily struggling its way North to escape its destiny of being swallowed by the Ohio, somehow the proudest. Not as wide as the Ohio, certainly, or as swift as the Allegheny, but almost independent in its easy sloth.

Not a ripple mars the surface beyond the lovers and the sparrow, only the green, brackish water keeping it from the somnolent beauty of a Vermont pond. A majestic tug, its power unseen but almost palpable, cautiously coaxes seven barges brimming with pyramids of shiny coal past the Point fountain, the prow of the lead barge finally bringing some movement to the water and scattering the sequins.

From the wall high above his head, the jogger hears the familiar tittering of the less industrious. Probably laughing at my legs, he guesses. In high school, a guy on the team had always called him "Sticks." But on this fine day of winter's death knell, he feels too good to even be indignant at the soft derision.

The jumbled lines of a favorite poem creep into his thoughts...."Oh, I have slipped the surly bonds of Earth and danced the skies on laughter-silvered wings...up, up, the long deliriously burning blue, I've topped the windswept heights where never lark nor even eagle flew..."

Probably oxygen debt, he muses, reaching the Point fountain where a dozen figures stand silent, their backs denying the frenetic pace of the city at work, to stare out at the confluence of the rivers. Some can probably peer down its length all the way to where it sacrifices its soul to the Mississippi and then tumbles down to that bawdy, painted-lady of a place, New Orleans.

The jogger, slogging now, labors past the aesthetics and angles hard up the muddy wharf that rims the Allegheny on the Downtown side and affords a view so suddenly and so remarkably different than the one approaching the Point that it snatches at your eyes. A fine idea it was to paint all of those bridges gold: Steel necklaces, they aren't. But the hue of fool's gold gives them some uniformity, a dignity they never had when they were various shades of soot and depressing eyesores that seemed to groan their way across the water to keep the city intact.

Seven or eight teenagers lounge on the gently sloping cobblestone wall that separates the Allegheny wharf and the park that rides above it. A pretty kid, her blond hair strung in two perky ponytails, holds court in an excited litany of you-knows and likes and wows!

One day an even, precise speech will flow from her mouth, the jogger knows, even if her parents have doubtlessly despaired of it. Led Zeppelin sings prettily from a portable stereo no larger than a steamer trunk, crouching precariously on the cobblestones, and the kids turn their faces up to the sun.

Ahead, a mud flat rises from the stones, the legacy of last week's high water, and the jogger aches his way up a flight of steps and staggers into the park.

Challenge time. The path runs uphill at a fairly steep angle and near the steps to the Veteran's Bridge, narrows to a funnel formed from the bridge's dank underpinnings and a rusty chain-link fence that hugs the bridge approach.

The long sweetness of the run finally yields to hard reality, passers-by startled by the heaving sound of lungs sucking desperately for oxygen. Calves turn molten, thighs tremble, small muscles scream.

At the top of the skinny path, rays of brilliant sunlight snake their way through the skyscrapers and spill down onto the intersection which marks the end of another day's sacrifice to clogged lungs and thickening waistline.

At a route-step pace, the jogger drifts back down through busy streets to Point State Park. People laze in the grass, here and there an infant, toddling beyond a mother's reach, turned coltish by even the slightest breeze. The lovers still huddle; those amused by the flapping legs and elbows have gone; the big tug is somewhere up the placid Mon.

An old man grapples his way off a bench, gets a purchase with his cane, and falls into conversation with an idler.

"Marvelous day, isn't it," the old-timer says. "Weather like this, winter can't last long."

Not long.

Did Thoreau so lovingly describe his pond because he was born in its shadow? Romantic to think so, perhaps, but doubtful. Still, within each writer, however pedestrian, is the longing to write convincingly and well about his or her birthplace. Or the locale dug the deepest in the heart. So, with the changing of every season, I would venture out to write about some slice of Pittsburgh or Deep Creek Lake, Maryland, a second spiritual homeland.

    Perhaps we're convinced that we know a place so well that our knowledge of it will sharpen to a keener edge our meager talents. Then, again, maybe this column was simply the product of the need to escape the office on one of those harbingers of Spring that renew the soul and defeat the notion growing in our bones on a February day that dread Winter will never die.

Daughters dear, you light up Dad's life this Yule

DEAR KERI and Kristi,

Another Christmas has arrived and once again, in there among the socks and shirts, I found that most wonderful of gifts, you.

Your love, which has buoyed me over a thousand shoals. Your smiles, which have melted the ice that sometimes formed on a flagging heart. Your health, the glow of which makes me humble before the gods. Your growth and promise, unfettered and soaring. And—thanks be to the good Lord who I am wont to forget on lesser days—your good-natured and continuing acceptance of your old man's numerous flaws.

As they say, guys, for all you do, this one's for you.

I could've told you this more often, but since the days of your birth, you have brought me the untrammeled joy which elevates fatherhood to the very pinnacle of human experience. Mothers, of course, may be permitted an exception to that. Nonetheless, I continue to believe it as firmly as Scrooge believed the ghost of Marley, scowling from the foot of his bed, would be his undoing.

Truth be told, this day belongs not to children, whom it mostly excites, but to fathers, who never fail to take from it that largest of all sugar plums, a matchless rekindling of the spirit. An assurance which insists that whatever they are or are not, whatever their failed dreams and lost goals and bitter failures, because of you, it does not matter.

Sometime this day, I will do what I always do, find a bit of privacy, nurse a quiet drink, and shed a tear or two. For many blessings. For things past and gone, that will not come again. Watching you unwrap a doll or stuffed animal, and tucking you in later, seeing you cling to them in untroubled sleep. For that precious mixture of fantasy and reality which turned your faces pink with pleasure and make this the day of all days. For tricycles and kittens and fancy dresses long forgotten; for the rainbow-colored clay paperweight which has sat so long and so brightly on my desk, bringing with it both order and warmth. And for making me one of the very few 46-year-old newspapermen with a fine collection of stuffed bears.

For those and other considerations, for yearly renewing my wonderment and my faith in the best of life, I've got some gifts for you that wouldn't fit under the tree. Among my New Year's resolutions—eat less, run more, criticize less, love more, and the like—are these:

Some additional tolerance for you guys. Of your music, Keri, which grates on my ears but seems to zing in your soul. I promise: No further comparisons between AC/DC and the Four Freshmen, no harangues that if you think Ozzie is terrific, you should've heard the young Elvis. Kristi, no more long lectures on how it is that I don't lecture you and gratuitous advice on how to run a life that you clearly can handle with admirable ease. Peace, my daughters.

I would also offer some extra space. Not distance, but the room to grow leisurely, at your own pace, without my carping, without my ambitions choking yours. The breadth to be what you will be, with the absolute faith that your Dad will ever be there; a refuge if necessary, a small beacon if desired. But there, as surely as there is a Christmas.

Though you might have some small doubt—I can hear you giggling at this—you may also unwrap a little package which houses the gift of paternal patience. Which, we all understand, is not necessarily in long supply where your Dad is concerned. Know that I consider your flaws as insignificant as single grains of sand in the Sahara, but that I promise to overlook most of the even perceived imperfections. Leaving the curling iron plugged in and so forth.

As best my instincts will permit, I also will try to give you more freedom. From my fears, my demons, so that they will not become yours; so that my horizons will not narrow yours. Freedom to take flight from my grasp and become more fully your own person.

To these, maybe I can add some encouragement to chase your wildest dreams. Rarely do any of us need an anchor, even one which cherishes us. Each in your own way is a free spirit. Fly. I will do my best to be merely the airport and not the navigator.

Time is the most precious gift, of course. I haven't always done a very good job in providing it. But, as was once said of a very great actress, "There ain't much there, but what's there is choice." So, I believe, is it with us. Still, be it resolved, more time.

Finally, I would give you what you have had since the moment of your conception: My unconditional love. Be secure in it. For however I occasionally rail or harp or badger, it is as unshakable as the heavens. The poet who said the single immutable law of nature is change, didn't know about us.

For me, you are the salt of this earth and a joy forever.

Merry Christmas,

Daddy

Divorce can wilt even the strongest Christmas spirit. So it was for the Musicks, father and daughters. Divorce merely separates adults; it tortures children. Especially at Christmas, when some of the pieces of what was once a family are awkwardly glued together in the interest of preserving, if not the joy of the occasion, then the illusion of it.

When Kristi and Keri Musick were preadolescent, we faked it pretty well. Christmas, or some part of the day, was spent together. Parents, children and step-children would gather. After a decent interval and the exchange of presents, we would, in sheer relief and delight, flee one another's company. Only cooler heads prevented us from celebrating the holidays by telephone or FAX.

In later years, the kids and I freely admitted, once in a spontaneous outburst, that we "hated Christmas."

For me, and for the girls I suspect, the day signified a feeling of failure. A second marriage, and what was in every significant way save legally a third, did not stand the test of time. With each ending, Christmas became even more awkward and fraught with the potential for misery under the mistletoe.

With the passing of time, though, we Musicks, a hearty if star-struck lot, have managed to forge some worthy Christmases and even our own tradition. It has to do with a seafood brunch and good wine and laughter and the bemused recollections of Christmases past, when Scrooge, himself, could not have held a candle to us.

If an occasional "bah, humbug" still passes our lips, you'll understand.

So 1983 shaped up as good year to come home again

IT WAS MANY things, 1983 was, but dull was not among them. As years go, one to remember.

For me, it was a time of change. A time to come back home to work and seek out some deeper roots, hone a little sharper my instinct for this town. To eat a Klondike and drink an Iron and feel a pulse that beats stronger here than any place else I've ever been. And agree that, yeah, for all of its warts, it's still someplace a bit special.

One sunny September morning, I stood waiting for a bus at the corner of Penn and Winebiddle in Garfield, two blocks from where I was born, and grinned until my face felt stiff.

"The poet was right, Babe," I told the lady. "Ain't no place like home."

Last night I toasted the changes and tossed down a few in honor of 1983, saddened some at its passing. Sang Auld Lang Syne a bit throatier than usual. As the man says, thanks for the memories.

Getting to watch Phyllis George take a bath, and wealth, and Robert Redford's looks, and a washboard belly...my annual aspirations...continued to elude me in 1983. But there are compensations for even the greatest of tragedies.

I got to watch all of my girls grow a year older and lovelier. The most seasoned of them managed it as usual, ever so graciously. "No. I'm not her father," I continue to tell her admirers.

Kristi and Keri Musick came one year closer to that dreaded time of independence from their old man, the realization of which also clutched the throat some. Still, they continue to grow in all ways and they were ever there when life had worn a bruise on this spirit.

So, too, did the other kids grow. Taller, smarter, prettier, wiser, and a little sadly, farther from the nest.

Life was rich and spicy and full in 1983. I found some sunshine, rode out the rain. Held fast when I had to, ran free when I didn't. Looked down from some mountaintops, up from some ditches.

There were good stories to write, in both the arena of sweaty amusements and the real world, into which four months ago I toppled, quaking and not altogether sure I was up to filling a very large pair of shoes left behind by Roy McHugh. But, salute the benevolent gods, there were fine readers, too.

I railed when I wasn't a McHugh; silently celebrated those occasions when the verbs and gerunds and participles miraculously fell together in sweet harmony and I could lean back, take a drag and think, "Got'cha that time, Roy."

I laughed a lot, cried my share of tears. Let a few people past the image. Drew love from some, who remain as steady as the sky, as perennial as the grass. Struggled with a new job and a new audience. You still out there, folks? Wandered and wondered. Saw a lot of new towns, new faces, new grief and wondrous new sights to be held firmly against those moments when the world turns brown.

As usual, I drank and smoked too much; listened and learned too little. Grew a year older and a few hours wiser. Tried to make some special people happy and didn't succeed nearly well enough. Dreamed some dreams. Hurt some, healed a couple. Flew to a few places where no eagle has ever been.

Just like you.

For a column writer, 1983 was vintage. When the imagination palled, the City Council cut-ups could be counted upon to shoot themselves in the foot. There was always a stadium sign or a politician with foot thrust behind molar to whet the appetite for the written word.

A few columns still hang in the mind, for there was no dearth of tragedy. A Kitty Conroy brutally destroyed and her killer laughing at a sentence that was an outrage. A derelict eating from a garbage can in the land of plenty. A harmless man with a dim mind, savaged for no reason at all.

So, too, were there triumphs to celebrate. A lady named Minnie, laboring nobly on that day set aside to honor work, as indomitable as the tide. Some pros one night in a hospital emergency room. The orderly passing of an honorable cat named Bo. Victories, large and small, by people of spirit. Just like you.

Happy New Year.

Across the years, some kind readers have asked if I had a favorite column. This was one of them. The poets say the only immutable law of nature is change. For me, the year 1983 was a time of great change. One family disjointed to create another, larger and more unwieldy. Love lost; love found. New job. New home. New kids. Everywhere, change. And, then, one column at the end of a tumultuous time, to try and get a lasso around it.

Somebody once wrote, "If the reach doesn't exceed the grasp, what is heaven for?" That, for me, was 1983. A turning point. Since then there have been others...no less confusing, no less daunting, no less demanding...direction usually determined by instincts too often flawed.

Some of those times and turns are described elsewhere in this book. This particular effort, produced from one guy's crucible, remains a favorite. Maybe because it might've been written at the end of any old year.

'You're as young as you feel' is more than a cliche

BY ALL THAT IS FAIR, you shouldn't be exposed to what follows. And, truth to tell, I'd head for the comics right now, if I were you.

But I have to tell somebody.

I...ah...have begun jogging, again. Uh-huh. Heard me breathing out there in Vandergrift about noon yesterday, did you? Yep, that was me, sucking air hard enough to curl my toes and making sounds that scared small children; a bumper sticker, "I brake for joggers," glued to the rear end of my old sweat pants.

Confession is good for the soul and, anyway, I hope to inspire the more sedentary among you with this tale of very modest triumph. I have met my alter ego in battle and that's him, lying over there in the corner with the lumps on his head.

It went down this way. I decided yesterday that if I am 45, I am not quite ready to accept a life of wheezing. OK, when I squeeze into size 34 jeans, my belly hangs over my belt buckle. OK, my hamstrings and quadriceps and back muscles screaming, I can bend over and touch only my ankles. OK, two flights of stairs and I sound terminally consumptive.

But am I not master of my own destiny, helmsman of my own ship? Am I ready to accept flab? Hey, has there ever been a company picnic where every guy there couldn't go to his right and come up throwing? So it is with me.

"Belly used to look like grandma's washboard," I was remembering yesterday morning.

"Looks like grandma's washtub, now," sniffed my alter ego.

"Just have to get back in shape," I said.

"Pear?" asked my A.E.

"Show you, turkey," I said. And just before noon, I pulled on faded sweats in the printer's locker room and headed outside for the old gut-check.

"Two miles, minimum," I promised myself.

"You'll be dead inside one," laughed the A.E.

I was so eager. So pitifully eager. I breezed past the noonday muggers and eased through Point State Park, the legs and lungs just fine, the years falling away with each stride.

Circling the fountain and heading up the Allegheny River wharf, I fell in beside a young guy wearing a hooded, black silk warmup jacket. I slid the back sleeves of an old rubber sweat jacket Terry Hanratty gave me 10 years ago and stayed right there with the kid. The competitive juices of an old high-school miler fairly flowed. Sweat clothes don't make the man!

"I'll run him into the ground," I whispered to my A.E.

"In three minutes, you won't even be able to see this guy," the A.E. chuckled.

Two minutes. Just as I was about to kick by the guy in the jazzercise outfit, my thighs turned to silly putty. From there, it was torture. I kept asking, "You there, thighs? All right, calves? Lungs?"

Just that quickly. I was dying. I knew how Lloyd Bridges felt every time the bad guy slashed his air hose. The back of my throat began to feel like a revolving door. My legs began talking to me.

"Cool it, jerk," they said.

In deference to their obvious wisdom, I shortened my stride and lumbered past a photographer taking pictures of the frozen Allegheny. My breath steamed his lenses.

"No pain, no gain," I gasped, noticing him staring at my stride, now as smooth as a flushed stork's. "Old war wound," I huffed and went on.

The long steps up to the Sixth Street Bridge offered either respite or challenge. I decided to run them.

"Good for the legs," I thought.

"Uh-huh, you'll wish you hadn't," my A.E. insisted.

He was right, again. I took the last flight on my toes, like a Prussian goose-stepper, and staggered across Fort Duquesne Boulevard, past the nightclub Heaven. Sweet irony, that.

Turning down Liberty, there were no skin joints to provide distraction and in my agony, I began fantasizing about a long, hot shower in the printer's locker room.

I hit the back entrance to the paper sounding like a beached whale and inched my way up three flights to the blessed shower. The water was ice cold. It felt terrific.

Moral of this column? I don't know. Maybe it's that you are only as old as you feel.

Today, I feel 84.

Let's see, the year was 1984 and this one marked my, oh, 15th attempt to get in shape. As they say about quitting cigarettes, it's easy, I've done it often.

The business of trying to stave off the affects of the advancing years through exercise is both endless and tedious. This particular go-around was successful enough, for a while. I got to the point of jogging six miles a day, five days a week. Cooled down with a Pall Mall, though. My belly never returned to anything resembling a washboard, but it ceased flowing over my belt like a waterfall and I no longer asphyxiated myself sucking it in when comely women passed by. Which, incidentally, I did to the point of making my forehead wrinkle.

Alas, several years ago, I recommitted to sloth, using as an excuse a troublesome knee. All slovenly men, I've discovered, have a least one rickety knee.

For those of you still trying to recapture decent physical condition, or at least lose weight, I've uncovered a marvelous new regimen. Change love interests.

Having done so for a fourth time in adulthood, I've gotten to know some divorce lawyers no self-respecting shark would swim with, but you do lose weight without having to sweat. Except, of course, when you're in court.

A lesson school won't teach: Dancing around the rules

CHEERLEADERS THESE DAYS seem to get fired for a variety of offenses. Some have been excused from their high school squads for being overweight. A while back, if memory serves, another cheerleader had her saddle oxfords stripped for mooning people from the back window of a school bus.

Now we have Tatia Zack, who no longer inspires the athletes of Freeport High School to greater glories because, over the holidays, she appeared in a Heinz Hall production of "The Nutcracker."

Ms. Zack got fired because she accumulated 22 1/2 demerits for missing three non-league basketball games to pursue her interest in ballet. Fifteen demerits is grounds for having your pompoms shredded at Freeport.

There have been protests, largely by Tatia's mother and some interested friends. Mrs. Zack says she's interested in "preventing future dismissals in case of such conflicts."

There have been meetings with Freeport Principal Fred Cummins, whose position on the matter is unshakeable.

There is a review of the situation presently being undertaken by Superintendent of Schools Dr. Edward Garlitz, who presumably has other matters a bit more urgent.

At last report, Freeport was surviving the incident admirably.

Uh-huh, a tempest in a teapot, lacking the sort of churl that was available in the instance of the cheerleader bounced for getting a tad pudgy. This is a tale without a villain, if you will.

By all accounts, Tatia Zack is a young woman of varied interests and talents. A member of Who's Who in American High Schools. Queen of Freeport's Sesquicentennial celebration. Class officer. Honor student. Rainbow girl. Three-year cheerleader and so forth. Who, incidentally, in two previous winters of calling applause down upon the heads of the Freeport Yellowjackets, accumulated nary a demerit.

By her mother's admission, Garlitz is an able administrator simply supporting his principal, whose decision it was to make of Tatia an ex-cheerleader.

By a third party's estimate, Cummins lacks both the intractability and defensiveness necessary to be an effective villain.

At issue, and what lends Tatia's travails significance, is a principle having greatly to do with the art form that is education. To wit: When it is right and prudent to bend a rule, even snap it in two, in the interest of a single student.

"This was a one-time thing, it wouldn't have continued," says Mrs. Zack. "I question his (Cummins) judgment."

Me, too. Although not his sincerity.

Asked if his decision had been fair and reasonable, Cummins pauses for a period of time during which the Magna Carta might be committed to memory

91

and is purposefully vague.

"The best answer to that is that the decision was made on the criteria established" by what seems to be a cast of thousands, including administrators, students, sponsors, etc.

"Beyond that," Cummins concludes the conversation, "I won't comment. Because I don't think it's in the interest of the young lady to do so."

They'll probably toss me out of the Old Newspapermen's Club for this, but I think that's a pretty neat position to take and Fred Cummins can principal my kids any time he wants.

Still, his answer begs the question: Should Tatia Zack have been tossed off the Freeport cheerleading squad for breaking a rule to which there seems to be a severe lack of exceptions, other than "illness, death in the family, doctor appointments, family vacations, impassable roads and car trouble"?

The answer is, any old way you want to slice it, nope.

Not if what Fred Cummins and the good people of Freeport High School are about is education. Which presumably has to do with common sense.

To be sure, rules are rules and kids should be taught that to break them is to pay a price. Ah, but what rule worth instituting lacks an exception? It says here that Tatia Zack makes a fine exception.

She aspires to become a professional dancer and has shown admirable grit in studying and practicing since she was 9. Daily, she treks from Freeport to Shadyside to study under what everyone seems to agree is a demanding taskmaster. Someone at Freeport must think supporting her interest is worthwhile, because she has been excused from academic responsibilities a few times in the past to dance. And being asked to perform a major role at Heinz Hall was no doubt the zenith in her youthful career in slippers.

Moreover, Tatia Zack is a fine student and without making overly much of it, apparently the sort of kid Freeport High seeks to produce with some regularity.

What she will carry away from being dumped as a cheerleader is not the lesson that if you break a rule, those in charge will get you, and damn well should. No, a kid clever enough to get A's in school will quickly learn to finesse her way in the future. Possibly by, oh, having car trouble.

What Tatia, and other bright kids, will learn is that she's living in a world of rigidity. Where past performance goes unrewarded. Where diversity of interest in unappreciated. Where an individual gets served up on a platter in the interest of keeping a debatable rule unsullied.

And that, in the very place it should be instilled and celebrated, common sense is a victim.

To every rule, a great thinker once observed, an exception. In this instance, no exception was permitted. Still, Freeport High School remains standing a decade later, Yellowjacket athletic teams have continued to prevail on the field of friendly strife, and Tatia

Zack has moved on to other and larger issues, her self wholly intact.

The basic question involved, of course, continues to plague mankind: When is a rule reasonably broken? When might the individual's circumstances outweigh the collective interest? When should a Fred Cummins say "rules, schmules..." and reuntite a Tatia Zack and her pom-poms?

Unfortunately, there is no ready measuring rod for these circumstances and, I suspect, they are generally resolved according to the mood of the particular time in which they occur. In the freewheeling 1960's, Ms. Zack would've perhaps been treated more leniently. The 1980s was a time—the financial markets a noteworthy exception—of some rigidity. The difference, possibly, between a Kennedy and a Reagan. Whatever, these days, as in those, we tend to be in thrall to regulation...to the notion that to create a reasonable exception to a rule or regulation is to bring about its eventual collapse. Still, we readily make an exception for, oh, Michael Milken. But a Tatia Zack? Never. Tatia, incidentally, became a professional dancer.

Vic Cianca's taking a few candid turns in retirement

THE WHITE GLOVES would beckon, fingers wriggling like snakes in a flour sack, imploring motorists onto the paths of traffic righteousness.

Yes, they would soothe the irritable, make that turn now, and thank you greatly for your patience and understanding. We will get through this madness, together. No, they would command gently, not yet, but have a fine day, anyway, and go in peace and prosperity.

The hands, always palms up, pleaded, placated, persuaded. Nijinsky and Magic Johnson between them didn't have his repertoire of moves; a body English that screamed instruction with even the slightest twist of torso or inclination of head.

Serious wrongdoers were frozen by raised eyebrows that fairly growled. Often, drivers would nod ashamedly, willingly accepting his rebuke. To them, when the frustration of the rush hour tested even his passion for it, he would bow sweepingly, sarcastically but, always, forgivingly.

There was not finer mime in this town.

The angle of his white garrison cap spoke volumes. And when he was on station, usually at 7th & Liberty or 6th and Penn Downtown at the height of chaos, the traffic seemed to flow like the Seine.

Alas, Vic Cianca, the Nureyev of the Intersection, The Cop Who Never Met A Traffic Jam He Didn't Like, reports that he is chafing mightily in retirement. Only Hollywood could provide a respite from its rigors.

Forced into relative idleness away from his beloved traffic, Vic has once more donned the white gloves that magically unsnarled traffic in this city for more than 31 years. And with style.

"It sounds crazy, but it's true," Cianca was saying the other afternoon, returning from the West Coast where he went as a consultant on the shooting of a commercial for Wrigley's chewing gum that required the presence of a knowledgeable traffic cop. In that calling, Gloves Cianca is the undefeated heavyweight champion of the world.

"I went as a consultant," he says, "but when the actors they had got out there with four lanes going in each direction, they were terrified."

A desperate director finally sought the Babe Ruth of the business and Vic says, "God Bless him, I felt like I was back at 6th & Penn. I was in heaven."

Since mandatory retirement forced him off the street 11 months ago, Vic has spent most of his time in a sort of hell. Imagine Kissinger without his briefcase. Fonda without her leotards.

"I was sad, believe me," Vic says of the Feb. 1 night that he hung up his whistle after working the 4-to-midnight shift at 7th & Liberty. "I had tears in my eyes when I left the corner. I was ready to jump off the Liberty Bridge."

In lieu of such drastic measures, Vic stored the white gloves with grace and briefly considered a run at City Council, where his skills could've found no greater home, after receiving gifts from his fans.

Without traffic to direct, Vic Cianca was lost. He considered becoming party to a pending lawsuit brought by some city police officers forced to retire against their wishes, but he couldn't do it.

"I'd feel like an Indian-giver going back after getting all those gifts," he sighs.

So, he's done the next-best thing. Going back for a few days at a time. The city of Erie had him in harness at a busy intersection for two weeks during Erie Days and he's done similar stints in Charleroi, Sharon and Latrobe.

"It's a shame when you can make more money loafing than working," he says. "But if someone said, 'Hey, Vic, jump off the 10th Street Bridge in your uniform,' I'd do it."

Vic Cianca, of course, is easily showman enough to have capitalized a bit on his 1964 appearance on Candid Camera, later voted No. 2 on the show's all-time list of favorite schticks.

"It's been coming along pretty nice," he says. "I give a little talk, show the Candid Camera film. They slide you a couple of bills."

Still, he misses the street symphony, the days when he bowed and dipped and smiled and waved and guided the traffic along as fast as it could possibly go.

"I wasn't soft," he says. "I'd put the gloves on with anybody. I kept discipline. But I tried to help some, too."

Pity there aren't some private traffic jams around.

One by one, inexorably, those things we call our institutions — identifying elements, really — have disappeared. Often, cruelly enough, in the name of progress. The Jenkins Arcade. Isaly's ...chipped chopped ham now sold, unconscionably, in supermarkets. Gimbel's. Stouffer's. And Vic Cianca.

A baseball pitcher named Darold Knowles once said of a hitter on an opposing team with a flair for the melodramatic, "There isn't enough mustard in the world to cover that guy." Vic would have understood. There was a little hot dog in him, too. But he helped provide this place with a bit of its style, a bit of its color.

It was worth driving around the block, even in 5 o'clock traffic, to watch Vic at work. The white gloves would cajole and flatter and charm and demand, and for a few minutes, the traffic frustration would disappear in the face of what was nothing less than entertainment. Right there, stuck between a Ford and a Chevy, knowing you were going to be late and have to pay a penalty of some sort...aware that dinner was cooling, or the kids were waiting impatiently or the boss was fuming...Vic Cianca could make you smile.

In his place now, we have traffic lights and cops standing on Downtown corners with thingamigigs in their hands to work the lights, and not a drop of charm to their name. And this is a duller place.

Corner grocer gave values supermarkets can't sell

"NATE..." MY OLD MAN would start, jamming his hands deeper into empty pockets, the embarrassment of being both broke and proud splashed all across his square, open face.

"Phil..." Nate Rini would interrupt, gesturing broadly with small, impatient hands that said "don't worry, get what you need, what are friends for, we'll carry you."

That's how we bought groceries when I was a kid.

Not from a grasping conglomerate hiding behind lacquered shills. On trust. On my old man and Nate Rini talking to one another with their eyes. A look that said, "I got the shorts this week," and another that said, "Why do you think you even have to mention it?"

We ate pretty good, as I recall, but times do change. Shopping then was interesting and personal, rather than only marginally preferable to having your toenails torn out.

For a very long time in the 1930s and '40s and '50s—until the supermarkets raised their ugly heads—Nate Rini ran a grocery store bearing his name just off the corner of Penn and Aiken in the lower end of East Liberty.

Nate didn't give coupons; you got faith and warmth along with the comestibles. Most of his groceries didn't have prices marked on them. Everyone knew Nate never weighed his thumb.

"Good cantaloupe today, Ruthie," he would tell my mother. She'd buy three or four automatically. It was understood that Nate had made a shrewd buy in the produce district and the price was fair. And not a feint so he could double the mark-up on the butter.

Sometimes my mother would pick up a head of lettuce and Nate would shake his head and say "tsk, tsk...little skimpy lately," and we'd have coleslaw that night.

Maybe a dozen Rini's would've fit in one supermarket. Nate's store was about as wide as a bowling lane and as cluttered as a teen-ager's mind. Stacked cartons fought for space with overflowing bins, customers twisting through the gauntlet between them. The flesh was necessarily pressed in Rini's. Neighbors rubbed shoulders and backsides in the narrow aisles, wariness and suspicion wearing away in the process.

On the bitterest day of winter, Rini's was a warm refuge. The shelves ran from the floor to an Everest of a ceiling, and hanging from hooks at various places along the walls were long poles with giant pincers at one end and at the other, a hand-grip that closed them.

Nate or Mildred or Babe or Mrs. Rini would pincer a box of Cheerios on a high shelf, lift it clear and then drop it into their free hand. Nate liked to catch the stuff without looking and through my childhood, I never saw him drop one box or bottle or can. When he did it, he would give me his tight, little smile and wink. I could've stood there all day watching him.

When the shopping was done, someone would write up your order on one of those little 3x5 orange receipt books, tear out the yellow copy, and slip the book back into a big metal rack that lurched lazily in a circle next to the bread shelves, creaking a tinny song. Every family had its own credit book. Ours usually looked like the telephone directory.

You paid when you could. And, Lord...Rini's delivered.

The supermarkets finally drove Nate out of business sometime in the '50s but if he is still around, he probably can't stop laughing while the giants of today's grocery industry squirm and shout and try to emasculate each other in the marketplace.

Nate didn't look much like Robert Lansing, the aging matinee idol fronting for Giant Eagle on television every 45 seconds. Giant Eagle, you'll recall, is the company that's given us Absolute Minimum Pricing. Which makes you wonder what the hell we were getting before Lansing took up the advertising cudgel. All Nate Rini gave was credit.

But Giant Eagle is a straight-from-the-shoulder outfit, just an out-sized Rini's, we are led to believe. No more coupons. No more weekly specials. Just old Bob there on the tube with his beagle eyes and shuck-and-jive smile, and AMP.

No sooner had Lansing struck than the other chains leaped to the attack, claims and denials and shrieks of unquestionable fairness flying in their wake. Shop 'N Save would retain its double coupons and it was lowering its prices, too. And anyone who didn't believe that could just check the five testimonial check-out tapes some shoppers produced to prove Shop 'N Save's prices were lower than Giant Eagle's.

A pox on both of you, fumed Foodland, which not only was keeping its double coupons and weekly specials, but was offering triple coupons on some items, so there. Us, too, yelped Super Dollar. Kroger, meanwhile, was trying to get rid of the last head of wilting lettuce before a strike.

Nate Rini would've loved it. He knew something that escaped the supermarket chains. The groceries will take care of themselves. Sell trust.

Rini's was flanked, in those leaner, lazier times, by a butcher shop and Schiller and Davis' drug store. In the former, all they really sold was meat. Fancy that! There was a big pickle barrel. You could smell its sourness through the plate glass window. Sawdust covered the floor, eddying against the base of the counter and smelling sweeter than freshly-mown grass. Kids tagging along with their mothers got a cold hot dog or a slice of what I still think is the best cheese I've ever eaten. The butcher gave credit, too.

On the other side of Rini's, Mr. Mehring or Mr. Schiller, the phar-

macists, treated the majority of the neighborhood's ailments. Doctors, then, didn't practice on golf courses and they would even come to your house, but there weren't that many of them. So when you got a cold, you went to Mr. Mehring and he sold you a bottle of plain, old crude oil and you rubbed it on your chest and on your nose, and you got better in about the same amount of time people do these days with antibiotics. The crude oil cost, I think, about a quarter for a quart or so. If you were broke, the drugstore put you on the tab, too. There was even a soda fountain that always smelled faintly of sweet phosphate and chocolate. You could spin endlessly on a red stool and make an ice cream soda last a week. But you couldn't skim-read the magazines on the rack until you had graduated from high school. Mr. Mehring ran a taut ship.

The drug store was a serious place, always quiet, the silence broken only by the hum of a slowly-turning ceiling fan. And if the store was closed and you got sick, you could always call Mr. Mehring at home and he'd come over and open up. And sell you some crude oil or aspirin or, for the truly ill, a mustard plaster. Times were a little different, then.

Your mother shows more honor than society will admit

NEWS ITEM: On Monday night, the Marion Center Area School Board unanimously affirmed the dismissal from the school's National Honor Society of Arlene Pfeiffer, a 17-year-old senior who in August gave birth to a daughter, Jessica, out of wedlock.

Dear Jessica,

Before long now, you'll begin getting lectures from folks on how you're supposed to be. How to speak and behave and, in general, how to conduct yourself in the symphony of man.

There will be no end of opinions aired on the subject, solicited or otherwise. Fortunately, there is a grace period and little girls 5 months old aren't subject to the expectations of others, save for occasionally sleeping through an entire night and not spitting up their spinach.

Before long, though, various people will attempt to shape your character, which by Webster's definition refers to moral strength. The thought here is that you will be best served in this area by listening to your Mom, who clearly lacks a certain sagacity but whose "character" as it pertains to moral strength must now necessarily go unchallenged for a while.

Growing up, you'll doubtless need a certain strength of character, because any community that dismisses teen-age girls from the National Honor Society for becoming pregnant figures to require a lot of the stuff from her offspring.

True, your mother erred. Probably not in the sort of moral sense that seems to have disjointed a lot of noses in Marion Center, but in the garden-variety area called common sense.

Getting pregnant at 17 is unwise. Not so very long ago, your mother was president of the student council. Even now, caring for you, she's maintained a 3.2 academic average, is 14th in a class of 164, is on the student council executive committee, and is vice president of the Science Club and the Future Nurses of America chapter. No doubt you are burped between chapters of "A Tale of Two Cities" and organizing the FNA chapter cupcake sale.

Alas, in many ways, your Mom is still very much a child herself and unsuited to your early upbringing, which is where the mistake comes in. A large and lovely piece of her own childhood will disappear in a welter of diapers and late-night feedings and proms unknown. You, my girl, are the weightiest of responsibilities life confers on us.

On the other hand, there is unmistakable evidence that you are fortunate to be the daughter of Arlene Pfeiffer, whose greatest mistake may prove to be geographical.

Not that being kicked out of the Marion Center Area National Honor Society is a particularly big deal, of itself. Compared with caring for and fretting over a child in the grasp of croup or a burning fever, the NHS will shortly pale into insignificance for your Mom and your grandmother, Cheryl, who, incidentally, seems made of the right stuff, too.

But the matter of your mother's character and leadership was raised by a five-person faculty committee not noticeably burdened by the virtue that made Solomon famous, and so it has import. That the school superintendent, John Mollino, saw fit to state in his discussion of the matter "...and I emphasize character" fully obligated your mother to defend hers. And, one day far down the road, perhaps teach you a valuable lesson.

Just your mother's fight to prove her right to NHS membership is a fair measure of character. Inarguably, it would've been much easier to abandon her membership and remain in the comfort of relative obscurity. Just as it would've been easier to simply abandon your life. As she said, "I belong in the National Honor Society. I have character and leadership. If I'd had an abortion or given the baby up, I couldn't face it."

What she obviously is ready to face is pressure and scorn and judgment, which in places like Marion Center can get heaped in abundance on a high school girl who gets pregnant without benefit of matrimony. And the suffering of which, with grace and fortitude, was once defined by a gentleman named Hemingway as the truest definition of courage.

No doubt your mother—in her uncertainty and the fear holding your future squarely in her young hands must surely entail—has her share. Or certainly as much as the grown-ups who dismissed her from NHS and then weren't around to publicly defend their position. Which, in some places, might constitute lacking the courage of their conviction.

Leadership, you will learn if the sages of Marion Center have not, isn't necessarily the high-blown element it's thought to be. Often it is an indefinable substance consisting simply of the capacity to leap from the trench and charge the enemy without looking over your shoulder to see if anyone is following you.

Character, though, is provided with a clearer, sharper measure. A lot of it has to do with taking responsibility for your life. Here—although it didn't seem overly difficult for some Marion Center faculty members—it is hard to fault your mother. She made a mistake, she is living with it, and judging by a photograph I saw, glorying in your presence. Which is as it should be. Of all the gifts, baby girls, I am convinced, are the finest.

Your mother obviously is taking responsibility for you and when grown-ups begin shaping your character, you might want to remember that a lot of good people, teachers and classmates, supported your Mom in a moment of deep need. And, perhaps, one day muse that she was wrong when she said, "They're punishing me because I got caught."

Chances are that's not true and that the punishment—a mean-spirited impotent slap of the wrist, really—was the product of a lack of compassion and understanding and wisdom. In toto, what you might call a lack of "character."

Good luck,
A father of daughters.

Not long ago, after more than a decade pressing a lawsuit, the former Arlene Pfeiffer lost her final appeal to right what she steadfastly regarded as a wrong. An appellate court ruled the National Honor Society of Marion Center Area High School shall forevermore remain safe from her presence on its rolls.

Doubtless young Jessica has learned some important lessons about those character traits called indomitability and resolve, as well as a keener appreciation of what it means to joust with windmills.

By all accounts, Arlene, who married some years ago, has led an exemplary life and Jessica thrives. We are, of course, left to wonder what the good burghers of the school board carried away from the incident. Did they take comfort in the goodness of their beliefs; the unassailability of their legal position? Do they continue to believe that they did the right thing in upholding the mores of their community at the expense of a young woman who made a mistake and then determinedly overcame it? Do they to this very day feel righteous and moral and fraught with that stuff they seemed to think at the time was "character"?

What might be said inarguably is this: A decade ago, the milk of human kindness around Marion Center had surely curdled.

Diabetes, 'old pins' take the fight out of Joey Diven

FOR A WHILE THERE, it was feared that Joey Diven would have to once more suit up, so to speak, but he's decided against it.

Joey would have you know that while he sympathizes with the plight of the beleaguered Oakland cops, his age, maturity and bouts with diabetes preclude coming out of retirement to protect them from Pitt football players.

The thought had come to mind that Diven's legendary services might be in order after a former Pitt player, Dave Puzzuoli, and a current one, Dennis Atiyeh, were acquitted Wednesday of beating up eight Pittsburgh police officers. Some of whom, incidentally, will undoubtedly have great difficulty explaining the verdict to the physicians who are still ministering to them 11 months after the fight.

"With my rotten legs, my fighting days are over," Joey was demurring yesterday morning from county Commissioner Tom Foerster's office, where he is employed as an administrative aide and to give the place a full measure of Irish charm.

Since retiring from the sweet science—street persuasion—Diven has given succor and sustenance as an aide-de-camp to whatever politician has been astute enough to employ him. While he is 1-1 as a candidate himself, votes have long followed Joey's various mentors around like a beagle.

Pete Flaherty was first elected mayor with Joey as his, in the Grant Street vernacular, walking-around guy.

"Pete can't remember a name and Joey hasn't ever forgotten one," says a veteran City Hall reporter. "Joey walked around in front of Pete and told him people's names and who to shake hands with."

When Flaherty ascended, Diven's reward for loyalty and unswerving good memory was unemployment. In time, though, Joey worked as a county detective, assistant to the prothonotary, controls inspector, parks employee, constable, and bodyguard to former light-heavyweight champion Billy Conn.

Once abandoned by another ungrateful pol, Diven smiled and said, "In the words of Gary Gilmore, let's get on with it."

In an earlier day, Joey doubtless would've gotten on with it in behalf of his F.O.P. friends. But as they say, the legs go first.

"I got old pins," Joey explains. "I'd have to get a ball bat."

In fighting trim, Joey Diven was 6-3 and 250 pounds of tough and willing. And known to work up a thin sweat pummeling whatever Pitt players were about, while worthier opponents were recuperating or otherwise occupied. Age—he's 63—and the diabetes forced him to hang up his knuckles.

There was a time though, about 30 years ago, when Pitt footballers would be seen skittering down Forbes Avenue in a cloud of arms, legs and lettermen's jackets. Shopkeepers wouldn't even look up from their tasks, save to note "must be Joey, again."

Folklore and eyewitness testimony hold that one season, favored Pitt lost to Penn State because young Joey Diven, in the process of becoming The World's Greatest Street Fighter, had decimated the Panther squad in an alley behind the Strand Theater the night before the game.

In those years, Joey was known as The White Knight of Oakland and was required, by reputation and inclination, to protect the rights of his neighbors against interlopers, student or otherwise.

The fabled joust—"I remember more than one," he admits—occurred after a friend, identified only as Abbie, had been in a scrape with a Panther. Not that Joey required any complex reason for a scrap, you understand.

"I think I put a couple of them out," Diven says modestly.

No less a meticulous observer than Press columnist Roy McHugh puts the number at five.

"I saw part of it," McHugh says. "It was on Forbes. Joey had this line-backer, Hal Hunter, bent over the hood of a car. Joey had a cast on one hand and he was holding the guy down with the hand that had the cast on it, and hitting him with the other hand."

In short order, Pitt replacements arrived and the engagement moved to the alley behind the Strand, where Diven hunched his shoulder blades against a wall and, in short order, proceeded to advance Penn State from heavy under-dog in the betting to no worse than even money.

"As I got it," McHugh chuckles softly, "he was taking them on in waves."

When the smoke cleared, McHugh recalls, Pitt was the worse for wear. "A trainer told me that two players didn't play and three who did, shouldn't have."

"It was a neighborhood, then," Diven says. "Italian, Irish, Polish, some blacks. Now, it's so congested. You need an interpreter. Everyone's Indonesian.

"The police had power then. They were feared. You gave them even a dirty look, they got out of the car."

When Puzzuoli and Atiyeh gave the cops a dirty look, or vice versa, a riot ensued, and it was almost one year and a thousand accusations later that the judicial victors were able to repair to an Irish bar to celebrate.

Joey Diven was there in spirit.

Pity Joey Diven never met Red Buck Tustin, the pride of certain parts of Greene County. Kindred spirits, those two. Among the larg-er-than-life characters who seem to have been leached out of contem-porary society, lest the rest of us be confronted by our own pallidity.

Red Buck would've appreciated Joey Diven's exploits, and vice versa. It is told around Waynesburg that one night Red Buck grew tired of simply another evening with the hops gods and thought to enliven things by having an acquaintance drive a 1955 Chevy over

103

his chest.

There followed some considerable debate as to the affects of such a stunt on Red Buck's well-being, but he would have none of it and a dozen or so beer-drinkers repaired to an alley behind a Waynesburg bar to conduct what at least one witness saw as "a scientific experiment."

Without delay, Red Buck stretched out on the packed dirt, and a conspirator slipped the '55 Chevy into low and slowly ran the front wheels up and over Red Buck's chest.

Accounts of exactly what transpired vary, but some eyewitnesses, to this day, claim that Red Buck skittered from under the car, brushed off his clothes and asked for a beer. Cooler heads prevailed and he was taken to the hospital.

"The doctor said he was OK except for some bruised ribs," says a man who was there. "The last I saw of him that night, he was sitting at a bar, drinking a beer. There were tread marks across the front of his T-shirt."

Red Buck Tustin has since passed on, but Joey Diven continues to fight severe diabetes to a draw.

Rolling Rock steeplechase surrenders genteel image

LIGONIER - I hadn't been to the Rolling Rock Races in 17 years until yesterday, but I'll tell you, the neighborhood has gone to hell. Old Judge Tom Mellon, who carved the original family fortune out of various people's pockets, wouldn't believe it.

Still, the signs were unmistakable. Beer-drinking. Out of a can. Couple of 3-year-old cars. Kentucky Fried Chicken cartons. Mangy old Labrador making romantic overtures to some red-faced matron's Russian wolfhound. And the most telling display of all: Damn, a pickup truck.

Break it to old Judge Tom gently, but his worst fears have been realized. The working-class folk have made it past that sign that warns "drive slowly, horses and hounds ahead" and discovered steeplechasing.

Used to be the Races were where the blue-collared went to study the idle rich at play. Oh, the classes mingled some, you understand. When a trip to the Port-a-let made it unavoidable, khaki and wool occasionally brushed elbows with velvet and flannel.

Mostly, though, the IIIs and IVs huddled in private boxes next to the race course and were kept a mile or so from the masses up in the grandstand. A $100 contribution bought even privacy for their automobiles. State cops handled the parking.

The Races were held in mid-October then, the Ligonier Valley fancied up considerably by autumn's splendor, a symphony of golds and russets. The unpredictability of the weather has advanced the Races a month or so now, but the gods were true to the purple yesterday afternoon, serving up the very first crisp hint of fall. At noon, plum-colored clouds drifted east into the valley, checked those private boxes and turned back to rain on Greensburg.

Once, the Races were a place of XKEs and Bentleys, silver torpedoes and cars that looked like 747s. Cadillacs blushed in their company. From their trunks spring wicker baskets worth not more than the Lichtenstein gross national product. No more.

"Things the same?" I asked an acquaintance.

"Well, they're still preppie," she said, "but here and there you can find a bowling shirt."

Time was not a woman at the Races would be caught dead out of tweed, preferably plaid, unless the weather was unseasonably warm. In that case, Rolling Rock became the home of the $700 tie-dyed denim pants suit.

Hate to tell you, Judge Tom, but yesterday's 45th celebration of the event was conducted in a sea of faded blue jeans. Some constants remain, of course. The only black guy around was wearing a three-piece suit and a strained look, Rolling Rock still apparently not an egalitarian steeplechase.

As per the custom, there was eating and drinking that suggested The Last

Great Famine would begin at sundown. Brimming wooden hampers and lace tablecloths for some; the ladies of the American Legion Auxiliary Unit 267 dancing attendance at the hamburger grill for the rest. Some all-conference boozing.

Lord, though, some guzzled Riunite. Been a lot of elbows ruined at the Races. Rolling Rock is one of the few places where you can wander about smacked-up and the cops tip their hat to you.

There are a lot of cops. State police, Ligonier Township police, Ligonier police, Loyalhanna Township police. Enough rent-a-cops to mount a serious offensive against the Mafia. Anyone going to hit the Ligonier Valley Bank, this is the day.

"The cops are all here in case the revolution starts," someone advises.

In time, there is racing. Three guys on horses, wearing scarlet tunics and those funny black caps that would look terrifically chic on a dowager, appear to signal the first race. The Ligonier Valley High School band plays the National Anthem. In the background, a horse neighs. Protest? Patriotism?

Across the race course from the grandstands, the official horsy set has already gathered. Lots of IIIs and a few IVs thumb through their programs, considering side bets.

It used to be that betting was a major part of the Races—"That's when it was fun," pouts a matron—but it is said that 10 years ago, Gov. Milton Shapp had a falling out with some Scaife or Mellon and put an end to it.

"Petulant little man," sniffs the matron.

Dapper bookmakers with hard accents and black bowlers would stand around next to state cops and handle your action. It was a hustle, of course. God couldn't handicap steeplechasing.

The horses, who generally look like they'd make passable glue, run two miles or more, jump various obstacles, clatter along at a fast canter. Occasionally one crashes the timber and a while later, there is a discreet shot fired. In the private boxes, they turn their heads away and all conversation ceases for maybe 15 seconds.

The jockeys are young and either daring or were dropped hard as infants. "These horses are all pigs," an Irish steeplechase jock named Leo O'Brien once confided to me shortly after being thrown from one.

The winning owners, according to the program, get "a piece of plate".

Presumably, silver. The jockeys get a little silvered old-fashioned glass.

The big winner gets the Grasslands International Steeplechase Challenge Trophy, the splendor of which attracts clouds of spectators. It is gold and purple. The Glassport Mixed Bowling League would treasure it.

Hard truth, the racing isn't much. The jocks stand in the stirrups all the way and the pace wouldn't make a $1500 thoroughbred claimer sweat. Much of the drama exists in the chance that a single hurdle might excuse the entire field.

Still, the Races are fun and worthwhile; benefit sweet charity. Just don't tell Judge Tom.

The first time I covered the Rolling Rock races, back when the swells and the working stiffs were separated by both space and the capacity to sniff properly as a means of expression, I drove an ice-blue Chevy. Parked it between a Porsche and an Italian thunderbolt so expensive it didn't need a name. My littly Chevy fairly blushed with shame. Still, I got to see how the swells lived. Saw a Mellon and a couple of lesser Scaifes. Ate caviar on a little cracker. Thought it both salty and pretentious. F. Scott Fitzgerald was right: The rich are different than you and I.

But, like the hoi-polloi, they are subject to the economic realities of their time, and so the Races became—of all things considering they were fraught with opulence—unprofitable. And, thus, went the way of all enterprises which produce too much red ink.

Presumably, the tweedy set returned to the private clubs to lick their wounds, charity the poorer for their retreat. And no more could be viewed Republicans at play.

A pity, that. Wonder what Old Judge Tom would think.

One dad's answer for sex questions: 'Ask your mom'

I'M ONE OF THOSE fathers who's always taken the straightforward approach to telling kids about sex.

"It'll make you crazy," is what I told my pre-adolescent daughters. When they grinned at that, I was forced to candor.

"Ask your mother," I instructed.

In time, there was no escaping my share of the responsibility. Questions on human plumbing were addressed in clinical terms. Household nudity was discouraged only when the thermostat turned balky or the doorbell rang. Physical affection was encouraged, short of any heavy breathing on the part of the adults.

Beyond that, I explained that sex was marvelous stuff, no more lethal than fumbled nitroglycerine, and was meant to be as private as a confessional.

Good kids that they are, my daughters didn't giggle at my explanations or inquire after the latest available information on the G-Spot, and we got through the experience as painlessly as possible.

Over the years, and as was appropriate, I've managed to discuss the nuances of sex with a variety of my charges without blushing. In my dotage, however, the task has befallen me again and this time around, for reasons which puzzle me, I am less comfortable with it. Perhaps owing to the fact that the questions are being posed by little boys, one of whom exhibits the curiosity of a Pasteur. Watching me scrape the blue stubble from my face one morning, he asked, "Does God shave?"

"Why do you think he has that long, white beard," I told him. "Go eat your breakfast."

All indications—he was recently detected studying a Playboy centerfold with something less than clinical dispassion—point to further discussions of at least the circumstances of his arrival. And, I suspect, considerably more.

He has never seen a stork, so I am considering the use of a recent invention of a woman named Carol Wells, who is either genius or fool. She is a sex therapist who has invented a game for the purpose of easing the plight of stammering parents who have just sat down to explain to little Johnny or Sue that "men and women are different and..." Of course, Ms. Wells also invented an adult sexual communications game called Bedroom Lingo, which sounds as though Richard Dawson should be present any time it's played.

The new game is called—probably to the everlasting horror of the gentlemen at Parker Bros.—Humanopoly. Park Place and Broadway are fallopian tubes. No, actually the center of the Humanopoly board is. The markers are eggs and sperm. Chips are earned for correctly filling the blanks to such questions as "when a sperm and egg meet, it is called...?" In fact, when they meet on the Humanopoly board, the game is over and the one with the most chips wins.

Ms. Wells approach seems flawed. My kids would probably be far less concerned with sex education than they would competition. They garden competitively: "I got more tomatoes than Phannak!"

Would they approach sex the same way? Would the little girls in the neighborhood then be safe? Is there a little league for playing doctor?

"We should get away from our euphemisms," Ms. Wells advises.

Swell. I know 74 euphemisms for human genitalia. Which of them would we all be more comfortable with? We got to the basic plumbing.

"Why do they call it that?" he asked.

"Everything has to have a name, right?"

"Why that one?"

Back to Ms. Wells. "We should get away from cover-ups for what we are," she states firmly.

Terrific. The basics, in fits and starts, have finally been covered without the need for Humanopoly. Can the moral aspects of the subject be far behind?

Shortly, the question of rights and wrongs, whens and wheres and hows, will arise. Humanopoly does not consider them—"it's up to parents to introduce that," Ms. Wells cops out—but I am already prepared for these inquires.

"Ask your health teacher?"

I have long thought that the best sex education a kid can receive is seeing Dad pat Mom on the ass and Mom obviously liking it. Beyond that, I tend toward ambivalence about sex, other than to hastily subscribe to the theory that in terms of pleasure, it flat beats the hell out of whatever comes in second.

About sex, I like what Ernest Hemingway said: To wit, what's right is what feels good afterward. That, for me, is an acceptable standard. If when your breathing has returned to normal, you still feel good about everything, you've done OK. I've told that to any number of teenagers in my charge.

The conventional wisdom, even in these unfettered times, is to talk about sex as beautiful. This, I suspect, is the adjective most-often used by those who, in terms of sexual experience, can't dredge up another, more accurate term.

Sometimes sex is beautiful. More often, it is fun; funny; dangerous; dull; lethal; exciting enough to wilt crabgrass, and, for far too many practitioners, a chore quite comparable to taking out the garbage.

Whatever it represents to you, it is probably wise to keep in mind an observation made on the subject more than 100 years ago by a British prime minister: "The position is ridiculous, the pleasure momentary, the cost exorbitant."

Thank you, JFK, for the imagination you awakened

THE PREVIOUS GENERATION had The War; the next, we must've sensed, would commandeer The Peace. What we seemed to have, those of us who embraced our majority in the very early 1960s, were piddling, limited horizons; a'narrow, tight-fisted scope; gripping ennui. Buttoned-down shirts, imaginations to match.

Chubby Checker said it all about us. We twisted; in place. But, in time, of course, we had him. His challenge. His style. His wit. His vision. Hell, even his peccadillo with Marilyn Monroe.

Maybe that's why today, precisely two decades removed from the pall of Dallas, the loss is still keen. And why, even if it is fashionable, we should not snipe at the ballooning target that is Camelot. But should hold firm to the feelings it wrought; its rich texture; its excitement, its colorful tapestry, its lingering promise.

There was a popular street term in that time: My Main Man! He was ours. Our Main Man. Our window on some better place, better time.

There is no intent here to heap yet another eulogy atop the mountainous pile. Nor to swell the myth, or impale John Fitzgerald Kennedy on the warts time has so clearly revealed. Or even to cast out a personal set of demons by recalling that crystal moment when we knew he was too soon dead. For the last one of us, that moment is forever cast.

No, the thought here—and writing about something else on this day is as impossible as eating corned beef on Thanksgiving—is simply to pass on a bit of the feeling he engendered in one generation. Mine. Perhaps in the hope that it will not be forgotten that for some 34 months, it was rich in freshly caught ideals and shone almost like a star.

We were the post-war kids, the Dull Generation. Lulled by rampant prosperity; hypnotized by an obviously untrammeled future. Reassured from even the oblique angles. There, look at Ike in the White House. Did that paternal visage not bode for the very best? Was not the great, unwashed middle-class dream right there for the plucking by any old engineering student or home ec major?

Our religion was resolute, plodding science; our God, the suburban-split-level-with-two-car-integral-garage. Our destiny was mediocrity. Tedious mediocrity, at that. Even Sputnik didn't particularly ignite our vision of the future.

In a dozen ways, with passion and with humor, John Kennedy shook us free of that destiny. At least for a thousand days.

When he stood before the Berlin Wall, grieving and fearful for what it implied, and roared in unhesitant German, "I am a Berliner," we knew. When the French lavished instant and unexpected affection on his wife and he identified himself with a huge grin as "the man who accompanied Jacqueline Kennedy to Paris," we knew. When a child and a dog crawled around the rug in the Oval Office, we knew. Cleave to this one.

His youth was ours and for the promise he held out, we forgave him much. The Bay of Pigs; being cautious at a time when just his voice would've helped assure the racial justice good men were dying for; his libido. As a visitor to his grave site said the other day, "The facts don't count for much."

So they don't. Not in retrospect, not 20 years after the fall of Camelot, not in the sweet irony of the fact that the innocence of a generation is buried in Arlington.

What remains is that he touched some wellspring in a generation. Represented us as a people better than we could have ever wished. Infused a small piece of time with fire and great, billowing hope. And made it markedly different than the ones which preceded and followed it.

If you didn't dash off to join his Peace Corps, at least you got a vicarious rush from the thought of those thousands who did. They were out there in the world stripping the lie from the Ugly American. They were evidence that we were, as we had been taught from infancy, a good people. And that we just might be, as he kept insisting, better than we knew, better than we ever had been.

That was what fell in Dallas. The sudden but unmistakable trust we had in ourselves, our abilities, our collective future.

And what we still feel for the loss of that, for the loss of the man John F. Kennedy, says much of what we might still one day become.

As fast-running water wears away rock, so time has worn more gloss off the Kennedy image. Time and tedious, tawdry books of pimply-faced infatuation with one man's sex life.

As a small torch, thinly-lighting the way to the future, Jack Kennedy has also been somewhat replaced, ironically enough, by a man from an Arkansas town called Hope.

Still, for those of us in our late 40s and 50s, Kennedy remains the symbol of a beacon suddenly gone dark. Alive, whatever else he was, he lent us at least the illusion of light on the path. Dead now more than three decades, he is but an annual whisper from the enveloping darkness.

Lack of men for Michelle Madoff shows city's decline

TO THE DEBILITATING list of bottomless potholes, and collapsed bridges, and rampant unemployment, and a subway system the length of a good-sized copperhead, and City Council by Ringling Bros., and a drop off in the quality of chipped chopped ham, can now be added: A continuing dearth of bachelors in whom councilwoman Michelle Madoff might conceivably take an interest.

It would seem there is to be no end of civic disappointments.

About a year from the day she did a passable imitation of James Watt by using the phrase "gutless wonders" in a radio talk-show discussion of the men of this fair city, Michelle has kicked out another rear molar in an interview conceivably intended to clarify her original remarks.

"You give me a man friend and I can line up 10 great single women for him in a flash," she told a reporter in the Post-Gazette. The converse, she says, does not seem to hold true.

Surely, though, a suitable man of wit, integrity, charm, grace and social bearing might be located for Ms. Madoff among the 207,729 males the 1980 census figures indicate are in residence here.

Of course, perhaps 70 percent of them have already been claimed by less-discerning women, reducing the field to 62,319 but obviously allowing for enough men to keep Michelle socially occupied well into her dotage and Elizabeth Taylor busy with the spillover.

Allowing, however, for the effect of the well-known male ego, the number must again be reduced by those candidates who remain put off by Ms. Madoff's earlier remark that she had to travel to New York City or Washington for a decent date. Figuring maybe another 20 percent there, the group's down to 49,856.

Just under 50,000 men would last the average woman a considerable portion of her social life, but in Ms. Madoff's case there are other factors to consider. Among them, she explained, is the ominous "double-edged sword."

One side cuts from the list all corporate men who do business with the city. Clearly, a conflict of interest would exist were Ms. Madoff to date a sales representative for, oh, American Bridge Corp. or Acme Pothole Patching Co.

It is obviously difficult to accurately determine just how many eligible bachelors must give up an opportunity to experience Ms. Madoff's social charms owing to her civic obligations. Hazarding a wild guess based upon the current number of inoperative bridges and the condition of city roadways, it is theorized Ms. Madoff's beaus must be shortened by another 10 percent to 44,870, still a healthy margin for the active woman.

The other side of the heretofore mentioned sword, though, cuts much deeper and, Ms. Madoff says, has been treacherously wielded by the news media, which has portrayed her as cold and unyielding.

"People (who) know me know that I have many other sides," she is quoted. "I'm a pussycat; I cry easily."

Credit the ink-stained wretches, then, for sorely limiting Ms. Madoff's opportunities for romance; the power of the press possibly having pared as much as 25 percent of the remaining contenders for her favors to a mere 32,407.

Utilizing techniques pioneered by the dating services, certain other factors must also be taken into consideration. For example, some men who do not like cats of any stripe—pussy or Siamese or alley. Subtract another, oh, 20 percent. And of those 25,927, doctors insist the number who are allergic to cats would run as high as 65 percent.

Right there, Michelle runs into some serious problems. Only 9,075 candidates haven't been culled out for one reason or another, and we haven't even considered some major impingements to her uncovering a suitable date without having to consult a travel agent.

Consider, if you will, the large percentage of men who have made too many other good women cry and thus are adverse to tears. I would estimate that perhaps even a full 80 percent of us have been cads to women at one time or another. Only 1,815, then, could be deemed worthy of an evening with Michelle Madoff.

But, sad to say, even in the age of enlightenment and sexual parity, there are men so insensitive as to scorn a woman purely on the basis of her politics. Ms. Madoff wouldn't have them if they were the last dates on earth.

"The point is that I am a good councilwoman," she says. "I am not only good, I am the best."

Faint praise, you may well say, but at a time where men must compete with women on the racquetball court and in the marketplace, her dedication to her tasks must take its toll among suitors.

In fact, this sketchy scientific study indicates there are only 182 of you out there who might serve as an ideal match for Ms. Madoff, a well-rounded woman who enjoys the symphony, art and gardening.

Of those, the Department of Elections would rule out, on the basis of current registration figures, about 30; and there is no question Ms. Madoff would probably dismiss those with no particular fondness for Previn, Picasso and posies.

Left, then are the two of us. Alas, I've long since been spoken for. Michelle will meet you under Kaufmann's clock.

In time, Michelle Madoff found Mr. Right, but in the process, lost the hearts of many of her constituents. After a pair of close-calls in which she very narrowly held fast to her City Council seat, she retired from public life in 1993. Prior to formally stepping aside, Michelle created her final controversy by continuing to accept her pay-check while living for months in South Carolina with her new beau and doing little for the taxpayers.

Fatigue and the strain of years at the public trough, she explained.

She had, she said, exhausted herself in behalf of those who elected her. So, for long periods, her chair in City Council chambers was vacant.

Tough, she said. The public owed her.

A year or so ago, she disappeared from the Grant Street scene. A suitable replacement surfaced recently. Rookie councilman Joe Cusick was arrested for punching a couple of cops while in his cups outside a cultural venue called "Bottoms Up."

And the show goes on.

Abandoned and ailing woman waits for 'what's fair'

SOMETIMES FRUSTRATION CLUTCHES Mary and her mouth gets so tight it turns into a pink scratch. She'll stamp a foot down on the floor hard enough to make the kids up on the corner jump.

She'd like to scream and break the furniture, but stamping her foot is all that she can manage.

Damnitall, she'll tell herself, she doesn't really want that much. But surer than hell, she deserves better than what she has.

Mary lost one breast to cancer and has to have the other removed soon. A knee went out and she had to have surgery. All but one of the seven kids have gone and he's about to turn 18. Her husband beat her up routinely and ran off with another woman and slunk back, then took off again for good. Her health insurance was canceled by a bureaucratic screw-up. She has a speech defect.

None of that is poor-mouthing.

She isn't sorry for herself. Not too often, anyway. Life is hard. She knew that when she was 5. Mostly, she's angry.

Bad enough, she says, being stuck by that miserable bum without having to listen to folks talk about how easy people have it on welfare.

Lordy, what she could tell folks about welfare. Every month, take that $260-a-month welfare check and stretch it so thin she can pour soup through it.

In her 50's, life has taught Mary a few things. How to finesse bad times, mostly. When she gets her $260-a-month welfare check, she pays the rent, $230, and "spreads the rest around".

One month, she puts the $30 on the gas bill. If she's paying, they can't shut off the heat. The next month, the $30 goes for the electric bill and she stalls the gas company. Be patient, she asks the utilities, she's doing the best she can.

The phone company—for emergencies, to talk a little in the evening—just has to accept Mary on faith. From time to time, she'll sell a few dollars' worth of food stamps to a friend to hold Ma Bell at bay.

Food is another problem. Mary hears about people spending food stamps for booze and cigarettes and sirloins. She doesn't know about that. Her $120 a month in food stamps are soiled and crinkled at the edges by the time she grudgingly hands them over. When she does, sometimes she stares defiantly at the checkout clerk, sometimes she looks away.

"I make do," she says firmly. And lest anyone misunderstand, "My sister gives me paper and soap to clean my house."

For now, the boy has to look after himself. She hates to send him out looking straggly, but he might as well learn early that nothing much is easy. He's on the street a lot. She worries about that. Be good if he could find work, but school is better.

Sometimes when she thinks about him, she wonders what she'll do when he's 18 and the monthly check is reduced. That embarrasses her. They don't talk about his father. What they talk about is money.

"I don't want to be on welfare all of my life," she says. "I'm very worried about my life."

And, when she can manage it, she is indignant.

She raised "seven children proper" and where Mary comes from, proper folks don't live on charity. They work and they pay their bills and they don't ask anybody for anything.

Welfare's the only way, right now, though. Still welfare and the other thing rankle. She worked hard all of her life and now this.

"I don't want to live high-class," she says. "I just want to go to bed at night and not worry about my bills."

The kids can't help much, and even if they could, that would be charity, too.

"I want no arguments with the children's husbands and wives," she says. "I don't think they should have to help. They have their own problems and, after all, I'm still married to their father."

Therein lies the rub. He ducked a long time ago and didn't look back.

For three years now, Mary has been trying to get some child support for her teen-age son. Not a lot. "Just something to help."

There was a routine, she was told. She had to file a claim. She filed. She had to sit through three hearings, she was told. She sat. She had to wait, she was told. She waited.

Finally, her husband told a judge he wasn't working. He was lying. Mary's still waiting.

"I have been a good wife to this man for 33 years," she says. "Kept his house clean, raised seven children proper. I think I deserve better than this."

If her health was better, she says, she would go back to work. For now, she frets and waits for "what's fair."

"This is no fun," she says. "I think the court should do something."

The Courts try, but now there are dead beat wives as well as dead-beat husbands, so the system is as badly-clogged as ever. Recently, for the first time, the number of wives who simply walk out and disappear is equal to that of husbands who abandon their families. A perverse sort of progress.

After this one appeared, Mary called to say breast-removal surgery had been scheduled. The guy who suggested the column reports she died sometime in the late 1980s: Still waiting for her vision of justice.

Girl in wheelchair could show other teens a lot

DEAR K-Girls,

This letter from your favorite preacher is intended to replace the soapbox. We all agree I am far too quick to leap atop it and I promise to store it up in the attic forever in return for the 10 minutes or so it will take you to read what follows.

On Friday morning, for reasons that hadn't crystallized in my mind and still haven't, I drove out to the Harmarville Rehabilitation Center to talk to Sharon Banker.

She's 14 and in her can be found all the good stuff I treasure in you guys. Easy affection. Trust. Grit. Quick, open smile. An emerging sense of independence. In short, she has all the potential for becoming a fine woman.

For Sharon, though, it will be tougher to realize that potential than it will be for you.

On a snowy night in February, she got a ride home from a friend. By all accounts, a good kid. Just like the ones you tell me about when I ask, "how are you getting home?" And you tell me with this neat kid. And I ask does he drink or smoke grass? And you roll your eyes and say, "c'mon, Pops." Or, "no, he's a straight arrow." Or give me that look that suggests I have just insulted your sense of responsibility.

I imagine Sharon's folks put her through similar inquisitions; received many of the same assurances that I get. Sharon's dad was probably tougher than you think I am. He's a policeman and he's in charge of O'Hara Township's drunken-driving patrol.

That snowy February night, he responded to an accident call. A car full of kids had hit a light pole. One of the kids in the car was Sharon. Her neck was broken and she is permanently paralyzed from the shoulders down.

The boy who was driving will be in prison for at least a year. He was stone-drunk when the accident happened. He'd been driving up to 75 mph. He scared the other kids by taking his hands off the wheel and pretending to be asleep and driving with his elbows.

One of the girls in the car, a friend of Sharon Banker's named Sharon Walkowski, finally made him pull over and she got out of the car before the accident. I would guess that was hard to do, causing a scene and maybe getting called a wimp.

I know you've long since gotten tired of me telling you stories like this; the ones that always happen to other kids. Lately, though, I keep running across them and it's tough not to think about you guys.

Maybe that's why I went out to see Sharon. When me met—she operates an electric wheelchair with her one good hand and the nurses kid her about speeding—I was more nervous than she was.

We made small talk for a while. She was in the ninth grade at Dorseyville

Junior High and a lot of things about her reminded me of you. She wears her hair like you do, Keri, layered and teased up a little. The nurses do it for her and I'd guess there hasn't been a prettier 14-year-old in Harmarville for a long time. She was a basketball player and managed the boys' team and was on the rifle team. She was wearing a purple top and gray sweat pants like you do, Kristi, and I told her you had managed the rifle team and I was always afraid you'd get shot, or shoot someone.

She laughed, but then we got talking about some serious stuff.

The accident: "I can't remember much. I remember the kid on whose lap I was sitting telling me, 'You'll be OK.'"

Her rehabilitation: "I go to P.T., that's physical therapy. And O.T., occupational therapy. And vocational therapy, for people thinking about getting a job."

The center: "I've been here since May 11. I'm the youngest one here."

The future.

She has pretty good use of her right hand and keeps a splint in the backpack hung behind the wheelchair.

"It opens my fingers," she explains. "So that I can do some little things."

Hopefully, there will be more and more of those little things. Her folks and friends see continuing improvement; Sharon is less certain.

"People say 'you couldn't do that before,'" she says. "I can't tell."

She said she was classified "a C-4 or 5." The difference is important. The people at Harmarville gave me a booklet and a chart in it shows that if Sharon reaches the C-5 category, it will mean she could possibly learn to drive and get in and out of her wheelchair.

But she's had to face some hard truths about not ever walking, and having to struggle to one day to be able to take care of herself in the routine areas such as eating and dressing and bathing.

"We're feeling that what she has now is what she will get," a social worker told me later when I asked how much Sharon's mobility might improve.

But she's a plucky kid and she's going home Oct. 25 for six months. Officials at Fox Chapel High are trying to find ways to make the school suitable for her wheelchair and her friends come to Harmarville all the time. They'll be important to Sharon in the next few years.

"The kids won't see her running down the basketball court," the social worker said. "They'll have to get used to seeing her in a wheelchair."

After we'd talked about some other things, I got to what had been on my mind. I asked her what she might say to other kids if she could talk to them directly.

That was a little embarrassing, but she said: "Well, it would change kids' attitudes if they could come here and see things."

Love,
The Old Man

About this one, there is little to say. What might've been was lost against a light pole in an instant. Lives were irreparably damaged. A future with possibilities yawning the width of an horizon was severely narrowed.

'War of the Roses' at an uneasy standoff Downtown

THE WAR of the Roses continued yesterday along Fifth Avenue, both sides entrenched and content with occasional sniping and patching wounds suffered in Wednesday's major battle.

The Downtown florists had withdrawn their heavy artillery—flower pots and plants—and retreated inside their besieged shops, while Gary Leventhal moved his big gun—an eye-catching flower wagon—to the rear echelon and set up a forward post with six cans of posies in a doorway across from Murphy's. In the mayor's office, they were back attending to less weighty matters of government.

Drawing himself up to a full 49 inches and smoothing the ruffles on his lilac formal shirt, Leventhal allowed that he had gotten no worse than a stalemate with the floral establishment since Wednesday, when the fuzz had wrought an uneasy truce.

"The chief inspector gave me one hour to get off the street," he was saying, as a man scrutinized his flowers, wearing a look that suggested he had recently wronged some woman.

Understand that the long arm of the law had been no less determined with the dozen or so florists who had levied complaints against Leventhal. They were under mayoral fiat to remove their displays into their stores, or to within a scant 12 inches of the front of their buildings.

"That's not enough room," Leventhal noted a bit smugly.

The battle lines were drawn when a dozen or so florists drafted a letter to Mayor Caliguiri, seeking enforcement of an ordinance that prohibits street peddlers from working Downtown. A rather churlish request, in Leventhal's opinion.

"Look, they might have to throw a few flowers away because of us, but they're sure not going to go out of business or anything," he says. "Everybody going up and down the street is carrying flowers."

That some were purchased from Leventhal seems to have irritated the establishment.

"The florists went to Mayor Caliguiri to get the vendors off the street," says Leventhal. "They've given me a lot of flack. And my boss has been doing this for 20 years, and they've been giving him flack since he started."

About three weeks ago, Gary Leventhal returned the fire. He moved his cart from outside the Jenkins Arcade, which is being vacated, to Fifth Avenue, within shouting distance of two florists.

The howling reached fever pitch in short order, but the public, as it will, seems to side with the little man.

"People come by and say 'stick in there,'" says Leventhal. "I'm just trying to make a little living. Dress nicely, please the people."

On this sunny afternoon, resplendent in red tux jacket with satin lapels, full beard neatly-trimmed, eyes twinkling, Gary Leventhal easily manages both.

"How much for the roses?" asks the guy with the guilts.

"Five dollars and tax," Leventhal smiles, the swirling green tissue paper in his hands neatly gobbling up the flowers.

"Tax? How about $5.25?"

"You got it, my man," Leventhal laughs.

Before the customer leaves, he pauses to acknowledge a bit of entrepreneurial charm: "Thanks, you have a good week."

"You, too, my man. You, too."

Gary Leventhal has been peddling flowers and charm on the street for the better part of five years. He came here from his native Baltimore to attend an opticians school and when "that didn't work out," he began selling flowers on the streets of Penn Hills on holidays.

A florist had him rousted.

"Another stupid ordinance," he sighs, high-fiving a passing acquaintance. "Guy's got eight shops, he's worried about me working five days a year."

A determined defender of free enterprise, Leventhal sells enough flowers to, oh, pay for a shiny red tux now and then.

"It pays the rent," he says. "This is good foot traffic here. We had to let our arcade business know where we were going to be."

For the time being, that will remain across from Murphy's on Fifth, although there are disbelievers.

"Hey, you goin' to jail, babe," giggles a street guy. Leventhal smiles and shakes his head.

"You have to go, you go the limit," he says. "I'll just stay in this doorway until they put their displays back outside."

The thought elevates him to a full 50 inches.

"Sooner or later," he says, "I know they'll have to."

Gary Leventhal is still around, still dispensing flowers and engaging small-talk to his Downtown customers. The battle between florists and the small entrepreneur ended quickly, although Leventhal later moved his base of operations to an alley off Smithfield next to what was then a Murphy's 5&10 and is now Sak's Fifth Avenue. He, ah, flourished.

Like the established street peddlers and familiar panhandlers and the street musicians, and even the winos who've been around long enough to be recognized by most passers-by, Leventhal brings the core of the city some color and flavor and style.

Periodically, churlish merchants register official complaints, or some dim-witted city council member introduces an ordinance to ban or restrict the Gary Leventhals. Yet, they persevere, in a meaningful way part of the city's history and tradition and stability. And, in the bargain, we get a charm fix.

Awareness group helps him beat anger instead of wife

IT WAS ONE OF THOSE steamy July days that make axe-murderers out of accountants.

The tension ate at him. Everything that could be going wrong, was. Sweat dripped into his eyes and plastered his shirt against his back as he tried to work around the house, simple chores made impossible by the frustration the heat was fueling.

The kids had been fighting. His wife and his mother had another of their rows, this one nastier than usual. Both bleated for his support. As the day wore on, the knot in his belly grew tighter and tighter.

Late in the afternoon, he beat up his wife, again.

"The heat...she was screaming at me...the kids were cowering in the basement...another hassle with my mother...I exploded," he says.

For 17 years, Al was a wife beater. "Since the week after our honeymoon." In that time, he beat up his wife perhaps 70 times.

The pattern was unchanging. His wife and his mother do not get along, their feud grounded in Al's sister. His mother is intransigent; his wife outspoken. Al is bounced between rock and hard place.

"I was forced into positions where I'd have to take sides," he says.

When he could stand the choice no longer, he took out his anger on his wife.

"I never put her in the hospital," he says in a small, even voice. "I came close. I set limits, but they didn't help."

For 17 years, nothing did and the pattern hardened. He would beat up his wife. Feel remorse. "Try to make up for it." Apologize. Live through "the calm before the next storm." And beat up his wife again.

"It was a cycle of violence," he says. "You blow up. Once, I sat down and tried to figure how often the violence was bad. It was several times a year."

No one could understand exactly why. Al is a mild-mannered, thoughtful, 38-year-old public schoolteacher who has never raised a hand to a student. By nature, he is "very calm." There was no model for violence in his youth. "My father never touched my mother."

"Where did it come from?"

Perhaps from stoicism. As the song says, "Big boys don't cry." Or admit emotion. For all of his gentility, Al was a macho man.

"I'd been taught to keep my feelings in," he says. "Not to upset the apple cart. For 17 years, I pretended things weren't happening. Then, I'd explode."

And wonder later if there would come a time that maybe he would kill his wife.

"Every time, I'd think I was going to have a heart attack," he says. "I'd read about one of those things in the paper and think, 'That could've been me.' It made me sad. I know now they can be prevented."

Al hasn't hit his wife since that steamy July afternoon.

"I made up my mind that day that I either had to get help, or I might do something to her or myself," he says. "I think about separating, divorce, but I have some beautiful kids. There's a lot of security here and I don't want to give it up. And I have deep feelings for my wife. She's a fine person."

And a victim.

Al got help from Dave Russell, who runs Second Step, an organization to help men who abuse their wives. It is an outgrowth of Pittsburgh Men's Collective, a consciousness-raising group.

"The hardest thing for me to do was sit around with eight to 10 men and talk about the feelings that led to violence," he says. "Even now, it's awkward. But if you don't talk about it, you get into the sort of situation I found myself in."

Al is finding his way out of that situation through Second Step.

"There is a commonality in the group," he says. "Everyone has realized that violence isn't the way to deal with your problems."

Not that the tension doesn't still often overcome him. When it does, he goes for a walk. Or pictures the look in the eyes of the men in his group.

"Yes, the anger's still there," he says, "but now I talk before I flip out. Now, I think I can handle myself."

A couple of years after this was written, Al killed his wife. Or perhaps he never hit her, again. "Al" wasn't his name. The interview was conducted by telephone to protect his anonymity.

In truth, no one knows much about guys like Al, except that sometimes, like O.J. Simpson, they wind up on trial for murder. More than a decade after this one was written, science hadn't learned much more about spousal abuse. Experts assured us after the brutal murder of Nicole Brown Simpson that the incident would focus attention on wife-beating and we would learn more about its causes and perhaps how to deal with the problem. We shall see.

Like O.J., people who knew Al would've been stunned to learn of the rage in him. That's what we do know: Mild-mannered men, and sometimes women, kill their partners. And we know that groups like Second Step provide an outlet for relieving rage. And, finally, we know what we don't know: Why spouses beat and kill one another.

Rich church unbowed by steelworkers' media event

OVER IN THE family burial vault, various Mellon ancestors could be heard spinning wildly while Dr. J. Robert Hewett was deftly pinching out the flame at the end of Ron Weisen's firecracker.

At mid-morning Friday, Weisen and some two dozen unemployed steelworkers had appeared at the East Liberty Presbyterian Church with a rather astounding request and were ushered into the presence of Hewett, the pastor.

Weisen is president of United Steelworkers Union Local 1397, the blacksheep outfit that constitutes the biggest burr under the international union's saddle. He is what in the Irish-Catholic neighborhood of my youth was called a tough, little Mick. Hewett pastors a church known for some years as Mellon's Fire Insurance. A silken-voiced welterweight, he was probably shocked to discover his historic church the focus of the angry unemployed, but easily was up to its defense.

The steelworkers had arrived—ironically enough in a bus supplied by the East Liberty Lutherans—with a demand that would've flabbergasted old Judge Tom Mellon, whose remains are located in the family crypt just off the sanctuary.

What Weisen proposed was simple enough.

The East Liberty Presbyterian Church, from an alleged $7 million endowment fund reposing in Mellon Bank, would pay every unemployed steelworker in the Mon Valley $188 a month.

"We're taking on the churches, we're warning them," Weisen had said earlier. "They're Mellon's religious branches. No church should be sitting on that kind of money with this kind of unemployment."

His argument perhaps theologically sound—comedian Lenny Bruce once said "any preacher with two suits is a phony"—it was nevertheless effortlessly parried by Hewett in the church theater.

The East Liberty Presbyterians—by historic definition "Republicans at prayer"—thanked Weisen for providing advanced warning of the steelworkers' visit through the media. Hewett certainly would entertain considerable discussion on the steelworkers' plight.

Weisen and chief ally, community activist Charles Honeywell of the Denominational Ministry Strategy, wanted a copy of the church's financial report. Hewett would arrange a meeting with the clerk of session to see if that might be possible. What about that $188 a month? Hewett would arrange a meeting with church officials in charge of mission funds. What about...? Hewett would guarantee a meeting on it.

Largely a media event, it fizzled badly.

The police sergeant whose cruiser was parked at a nearby corner did not feel constrained to put in an appearance. The one TV camera crew in attendance was at pains to stay awake. A curious reporter familiar with

Presbyterian legerdemain did not stay long. And the strategy was painfully obvious—Presbyterians would simply out-meeting the Steelworkers. Weisen and his doughty band piled back on their bus and headed for the next rich church on the list and more keen disappointment.

Their idea is certainly novel: Churches of grandeur, built by the rich, should by dint of belief undertake to ease the burdens of the less-fortunate. Strapped by a certain naivete, Weisen also wants the banks to adopt a conscience.

Feisty enough, he flails at no end of targets. Mellon Bank: "A neighbor you can count on? Don't bank on it!" The international union, which he pillories with a rich contempt. His arch-enemy, USW President Lloyd McBride, for whom his highest praise is "lackey." Apathetic steelworkers who don't want to fight.

"It's going to get bloody," he says of the steelworkers' current confrontational policy. "It has to."

If much of what Weisen has to say smacks of rhetoric—the impression is inescapable that he's as much interested in struggle as solution—there is one possibility. Angry men might just listen to him. He beats hell out of union leadership platitudes and Mahatma Ghandi was once a voice in the wilderness.

"I'm not a wild man," Weisen is arguing in his office at Local 1397, housed in a dusty buff brick building in Homestead, across the street from a Mellon branch office. "I'm just telling the truth."

Ron Weisen's truths are these:

• The international union is in bed with the industry giants: "They've forgotten how to fight. They've been sleeping with the companies so long they ought to get maternity rights."

• Mellon—"Mellon the Felon"—is investing too much money in foreign countries, too little in the Mon Valley.

• Whatever relief the unemployed steelworkers are to get, they'll have to find it on the streets.

It says here the steelworkers visit to the churches, if sadly ineffective and mindful of Don Quixote tilting with windmills, was timely. Something to perhaps remind the affluent at prayer this morning that the Lord they worship had only one suit. And no union leadership should be without a gadfly. And for all of Mellon's sophisticated public explanations, the fact is the bank had record earnings a year ago and could be taking a larger role in solving the steel crisis in the Mon Valley. The Mellon vice president who said Thursday the steel companies should come to the bank if they need help probably leans on a mahogany bar with a U.S. Steel vice president or two on occasion.

"We're going to take on the international and we're going to have a revolt," Weisen says. "We're going to take on the banks and the politicians and the government."

Combined, they probably won't prove as tough as the Presbyterians.

The banks and the politicians and the international union, and even the Presbyterians, proved too resolute and uncompromising for the Ron Weisens, of course, and ultimately all the DMS—and its' successor, the DMX—did was make a lot of noise and deposit a few rotting fish in some safety-deposit boxes at a Mellon Bank branch or two.

Two years or so after this was written, the floodwaters had passed well over the head of the ineffective protest movement perhaps best characterized by Ronnie Wiesen, the tough, little Mick who wasn't nearly tough enough.

In fact, there was no revolt and, quite soon, all the consciences of those who presided over the downfall of the steel industry here seemed well-salved.

The players in the movement have scattered. Ron Weisen's son was paralyzed in a diving accident and was treated in Russia at a facility specializing in spinal injuries. Honeywell faded from public view along with the other more prominent activists, including the Rev. Douglas Roth, and the movement has not so much died as it has dissipated into meaninglessness. And in the mills along the rivers that once sent flames shooting a hundred feet into the night skies, balls of dead brush whisk slowly through the still shadows.

B-grade script held real terror for bank manager, wife

IT'S ONLY supposed to happen on television. The plot is threadbare and weary; even the roles as worn as a nun's knees:

Bank robbers, manager with kids feeling as vulnerable as hell, G-Men hot on the spoor, wife desperately afraid for her family. Roll tape. Cue the dirge music. Holdup thwarted. Bad guys flee in a blaze of gunfire. What they call in the trade a B movie. Paramount hasn't been interested in such fantasy for decades.

Frank and Debbie Ferra lived it for two weeks. A nightmare with a happy ending, maybe, but your fingernails would be gone if you'd been around while the action was unfolding.

Every day for about two weeks, manager Frank Ferra would glance out the front window of the Black Lick branch of the Homer City State Bank and across busy Route 119 at the Burrell Elementary School. The hair on his neck would rise. His two kids go to school there. Stray gunshots from a bank stickup and...

Every day for two weeks, Debbie Ferra never strayed far from the telephone and sat and waited for 9-year-old Brian and his 6-year-old sister, Diane, to get home from school. When they did, she started breathing again. "But it still felt like there was a heavy weight in my chest."

Every day for two weeks, what the Ferras mostly did was just wait. For the Homer City State Bank to be hit. For reassurance their children would be safe. For relief from the tension. Yesterday morning at 11 a.m., the waiting was over. You could've heard Debbie Ferra sigh in Punxsutawney.

"It's been a living hell," she was telling a reporter, trying to steady her tone the way people do when they're being interviewed for the first time, and not getting anywhere even close.

"I felt like I was a prisoner in my own house," she was saying, the sentences sounding as though they were being jerked from her throat. "I don't feel the children have been safe. There was a constant worry for the other children they play with. It's been very trying."

Couldn't have been anything else since the day the FBI agents showed up in Black Lick a fortnight ago and told Frank Ferra not to get excited, but his bank figured to be a target. Precautions were taken. Everyone waited some more. The situation had a certain Mack Sennett overtone. Robbers case bank, FBI men trail robbers. Trap is baited. Bad guys lured, trussed up, quickly packed off to the slammer. Almost worked out that way. Almost.

"They followed them around and followed them around and followed them around," Frank Ferra says of the FBI tracking the suspects. "Finally, they made their move."

For Frank and Debbie Ferra, the ticking was silenced.

"It's been like sitting on a time bomb and waiting for it to go off," Frank Ferra was saying early yesterday afternoon while FBI agents and the state police were sealing off a cornfield to which two of three bank robbers who'd attempted to hold up the Homer City Bank had fled. "Basically, it's been going on for a couple of weeks."

There is, Ferra says, a rule of thumb for bank managers in such situations.

"You tell your wife, you don't tell your kids," he says. "But I didn't want them ever left alone. You don't know what you're dealing with."

His imagination offered some chilling speculation.

"What if somebody grabs them and says 'Give me everything in the bank or I'll kill your kids?'" Frank Ferra asks.

What if? Run a small-town, rural bank, the options are few. Mostly, you don't think of anything else, you and your wife don't talk about anything else, and you hope to hell the cops know exactly what they're about.

"The FBI had a surveillance team working," Ferra says. "They had a kind of feeling this bank was going to be hit. A couple of suspects were driving around here. There was a hint this would be the bank.

"It proved out."

By the time it did, Frank Ferra, the other employees and some customers had been locked in a room in the bank basement; the FBI was upstairs greeting the robbers. Some shots were exchanged, the chase was on, one suspect was arrested. And the bomb under the Ferras quit ticking.

"For a while," Debbie Ferra says, tension still commanding her voice. "You always live under a shadow. Will you get a call that your husband's been shot...your kids..."

Frank Ferra's been the Homer City banker for a dozen years. The threat of a holdup is as much a part of his business as wrinkled $1 bills and farmers borrowing against the next crop.

"Oh, my, there are so many things that run through your head," he says. "You think of your family. Who's following you around. Worry about your children. A hostage situation."

A hostage situation. Now there's a neat plot twist for you. Very popular these days. But bank managers and their families living under the gun...old stuff. Quit making those back in the days of, oh, J. Edgar Hoover.

The Homer City State Bank, Black Lick branch, has since become part of the S&T Bank system, Burrell branch, and it is one of several that Frank Ferra oversees as an S&T supervisor. Theoretically, anyway, his personal vulnerability has lessened.

Once fascinated with the plots involving bank robbery—Frank Sinatra starred as a convincing psycho holding a banker's family hostage in a 1960s film called "Suddenly"—Hollywood hasn't been interested in such movies for years. Too unbelievable.

Banks, of course, remain popular with the bad guys. And people like Frank and Debbie Ferra continue to live with fears the rest of us can't really appreciate.

When it came to cards, Mechanic held winning hand

RICO THE BAKER and Billy the Pourer were reminiscing the other day about The Mechanic, who deals only azaleas these days, but once was considered a genius because people could hear the cards in his hand purring.

In The Mechanic's day—1950s to early '70s—you could get a bet down in this town on anything from five-card draw to whether it might rain in Rangoon the following afternoon at 4 o'clock.

In maybe a dozen bars, only girls who took their clothes off were comparable attractions to the poker games in the back room. For years, the action was so heavy in a Barbout game on Broad Street in East Liberty that cops would sit outside in a squad car to protect the players from being hijacked. The Mechanic—who did not trust dice and thus disassociated himself from Barbout—was in those years revered.

"The very best," sighs Billy, who is called The Pourer because it is said that if it can be poured, Billy will drink it. "I seen a lot of them come and go. None of them was slicker than him. He could've put an ace of spades in a cobra's mouth."

Rico the Baker is quick to agree, The Mechanic having once provided him with a vacation in Aliquippa.

"I am holding a grand the day before going on a trip, but I happen to have this thing about a girl singer in an after-hours joint in Oakland," Rico explains. "So, I go to the club where she works and in the back, there is a game. While I am waiting for the singer, I decide to sit in. I make a big mistake."

Rico grew up not far from New Kensington, which at the time of his youth was the national capital of poker, craps, church bingo and applying steam irons to the feet of welshers. He was not unfamiliar with five-card stud at age 4. But Rico had then to make the acquaintance of a world-class dealer.

The Mechanic was a silent, slender guy whose face you would not remember if he ran off with your wife. In those days, he was plying his craft in various East Liberty card emporiums.

"This one night, he gives me an education and afterwards maybe I show him one trick he hadn't seen," says Rico the Baker, who is called that because he is Italian and because when, on those occasions when he cannot make a connection, he finds solace in kneading dough. "Anyhow, he gets the grand before the blonde finishes her first set and there goes my vacation.

"But he is a nice guy and I tell him he has wrecked my trip and he lends me $500. I figure out what happens to me the next day, I decide to consider it a gift and I never go back."

Billy the Pourer, who drinks with Rico, just smiles. The Mechanic, he maintains, was a man of such rare distinction in his craft that few of his lambs ever realized they had been shorn.

"He never give anyone even a sniff of his game," Billy says, "but he could make the cards talk. You got a 10-high straight, he pulls a jack-high. You are holding trip 3s, he has 4s."

"He was the classic definition of one-upmanship," Rico the Baker notes. "He loses once every Hailey's Comet."

Except to Dapper Jack, The Baker is reminded.

"Yeah, except for Jack."

A tall thin boulevadier who always wore a stickpin, Jack was said to have owned but one shirt and a $10 bill, and never found a reason to change either.

"The day he died, they found the first dollar he ever had clenched in his hand," says The Pourer, who once roomed with Jack and claimed the only problem with the arrangement was "having to take a shower with my wallet in my hand."

Jack has departed, but The Mechanic can be found in idyllic retirement. In his 70s, he mostly tends his small flower garden and dabbles in solitaire.

"He always wins," Billy explains. "He couldn't never break the habit."

His grand reputation in these parts remains intact, although The Mechanic's chief place of business—a bar owned by his brother, the cop—is now a Dairy Queen. "He could make a jack wink and a queen simper," sighs Billy.

"What he had was patience," says Rico the Baker. "And timing. Never just turned out a guy's pockets. The little pots, he give you. The big ones, he twisted your heart out."

Not that The Mechanic was without a romantic side, although it rarely surfaced.

"Your kid was making her First Communion, he wouldn't take your money," Billy the Pourer insists. "And what about The Croaker?"

It was The Croaker who finally brought out The Mechanic's compassion. The Croaker is now a very well-known keeper of a Downtown saloon, where they specialize in drinks that make your eyeballs roll up in your head and your nose go numb.

One night the week he was to be married, The Croaker sat down in a game The Mechanic was running and before long, he was arm-weary from dragging in the money. A friend quietly suggested that it was time to leave.

"Leave? You nuts? I am on a roll!" The Croaker tells the friend.

"No," says the friend, "you have just gotten a wedding present."

The other night, a dozen years after he was trimmed by The Mechanic, Rico ran into the after-hours songbird.

"We are trying to figure out exactly what year we met," he says. "I start talking about blowing my vacation. She says, 'Now I remember, you were one of The Mechanic's dummies.'"

Billy the Pourer has been dead for a while. It is said that his liver, which got to be the consistency of an old catcher's mitt, finally gave out on him. The Mechanic is dealing in whatever locale the Lord reserves for guys who could make playing cards sing arias. The Croaker, a thinly-veiled disguise for a well-known saloon owner, flourishes. His raspy voice continues to make bar napkins quiver.

Rico the Baker is, in a manner of speaking, off the board.

About six years ago, in a decision that still shocks his intimates, he gave up both booze and his incredibly-successful pursuit of the opposite sex, who, to a woman, believed him to be Pernell Roberts, a television actor. His health has improved, he has become fascinated with his expensive home audio system, and he remains what he was when I was writing about him but could not for obvious reasons identify him: An important union official.

Labor Day like all others to Homewood woman— a time to work

At mid-afternoon on the day given over to the consecration of sweat, Organized Labor dragged a chair to the front door of her neat house on Bennett Street in Homewood for a breath of air.

Organized Labor, in this instance, is a fine, gentle lady of considerable years named Minnie Hopkins, who knows more about the stuff than Samuel Gompers or the combined membership of the Longshoremen's Union ever dreamed of.

While the day rang with cries of the dignity of labor, the merit of labor and the virtue of labor—invariably saluted at picnics by folks in Bermuda shorts—Minnie Hopkins honored it by working. She would, she explained, return to her formal job the next morning.

"Just calling around gettin' the gossip," she explains the short break during her day of rest. In time, she would clean house, cook for herself, bake corn-bread for a client, receive a caller, move furniture in anticipation of the painters, weed the flower garden, help her upstairs roomer get ready to move, wash clothes and, in the Pittsburgh manner, "redd up."

She was, she said, glad to have the day off, "with pay."

While labor was parading and picnicking and verbally shredding Ronald Reagan and whatever other Republican was handy, Min Hopkins was doing what she has been doing deep into the eighth decade of her life, working. And, she said, enjoying the hell out of it.

"Oh, yeah, honey, I've worked pretty hard," she was saying, tugging down onto her brow a do-rag, floppy and faded, that spoke volumes. "Always have. Like to. Although I can't do what I could."

What Minnie Hopkins could once do was enough work to make strong men faint. She raised two sets of kids, hers, and for 11 years, the three children of a New York City doctor. For two decades, she took care of her bedridden mother, who died a year ago at 90. She cooked for a living. She owned a couple of beauty parlors. And over the years, what she hasn't scrubbed never got dirty.

"Used to be so ashamed of day work," she laughs of the long-ago time when her vanity outweighed her appreciation of honest toil. She is a story-teller, Min Hopkins is, her experiences rolling forth in a soft voice laced with gentled vowels and weariness. But she likes to talk, so she tells one on herself with that rich, self-mocking chuckle that only the old can bring to bear on themselves.

"You know the 60 streetcar used to run out this way and then on over to Shady?" she says. "Well, those days, people didn't want no mop on their porches. They wanted knee work. I was so embarrassed to have my friends see me down there on my knees, so every time I'd see the 60 coming down the street, I'd find something to do in the house." She pauses to laugh.

"Foolishness, it was."

Well over a decade beyond Social Security, Minnie Hopkins still works for a living. Five days a week. For $2 an hour and $1.20 lunch money.

Her retirement is not imminent. "Goin' to do it long as I can still hop around," she says.

The inner-city community center that employs Minnie Hopkins provides her with transportation to and from work by van. When the van breaks down, which it does with the regularity of a metronome, she takes three different buses to her clients in Hazelwood. Often she climbs hills—"I can work, but I can hardly take those hills"—because she thinks her supervisor doesn't know she has a heart condition. Once, stuck in Hazelwood at the end of the day, she hitchhiked back to Homewood.

She is what is called a senior companion, which means she does for old people. Does meaning whatever they need done. "And prettying up for them," Minnie adds.

"She is a giver," says the supervisor.

"Five senior ladies," Minnie Hopkins explains. "I can't keep them alive, but I watched my Mama die and I do the best I can for them. Father's gone, Mama's gone, my son's gone...sometimes I get the blues so bad I just take to crying. That's why I took this job, to have something to do.

"Got five senior ladies...three white, two black."

All in need.

There is Monday, "Blanche is Mondays, although she gets so lonesome, sometimes I go by Saturday."

There is Tuesday, who shares the first floor of an old house in Hazelwood with some nesting birds. "She didn't have no homemaker, so I took that job, too."

There is Wednesday. "I cook for her a little. Clean her floors because they get nasty."

Thursday is bed-fast. "My Thursday lady really needs help," Minnie Hopkins says. "She's lonely. She likes me to eat with her, so I do, even when I don't want to. And I read to her."

And bake her a rum pie.

"Shame those old people can't get what they like to eat," says Min, who makes a note to go out "for fresh string beans. And Downtown to Donahoe's to get her a streak of lean sidemeat."

And bathe her. "She can't get into a tub, so what I do is pan-bathe her."

Friday will need her feet washed this week.

"I told her, 'I'm goin' to scrub those feet cleaner than they've ever been in your life.'"

Minnie...Happy Labor Day.

The iron imperative in this place is getting it done. You can talk about it, or not, as you choose. Explain it, or not. Brag on it or keep your mouth shut. But around here we understand the folks at Nike who implore, "Just do it!" And we give short shrift to anyone failing to get the job done or the task completed. Usually those who demonstrate incompetence or a lack of grit necessary to finish a piece of work are referred to as "jerk-offs." The thoughtful will comprehend the deepest meaning of that dismissive term.

The late Min Hopkins got it done. Usually in behalf of someone else.

30 years pass by, but the devilish spirit is still alive

HE IS 46 now, the ballast of my youth. Largely untouched by the years that have begun chiseling ravines along my cheeks and threatening my belt buckle.

An eon ago, we were slick and strong. I was slick; he was strong. In times of decision and trouble—now they seem few, then as numerous as stars—his gut instinct was to look to me. Mine was to screw up. He was always around to pick up the pieces.

Want to grab a beer out of Delituso's cooler?

What if we get caught?

We won't.

We did.

Cop: Who's idea was it? Two voices: "Mine."

As hard as it is for me to accept—and graying chest hair is not harder—that was 30 years ago. In a time as different from this one as the Four Freshmen and Led Zeppelin. Still, the indomitable ties of boyhood have successfully weathered the transition.

So we discovered over lunch Friday after exchanging that honored lie: You haven't changed at all. Much of the time was spent with that ageless game of freshly redeemed friendship, "Remember when...?" Whatever awkwardness we felt disappeared in a handshake.

A drink seemed called for, so we drank a toast to what was. Old habit, that. When we were dashing pell-mell through the teen-age maze, we'd sneak a couple of Irons and tap the cans together and grin at one another from somewhere deep in the security that, if we were singly trapped in the wretched vulnerability of adolescence, together we were invincible.

That security has outlasted the years, and the changes, and having entire decades pass when we couldn't remember the names of the other's children. Still...remember when we swaggered the East End streets, uncertain of nothing on the face of the Earth save for the prospect of Friday night's movie date with those bombshells from Brushton, red-haired Eileen and blonde Pat? Oh, yeah, we remembered, their loveliness embellished a hundredfold by the passing of time.

Remember?

Who could forget? His Dad, driven deep into the bottle by his mother's death, propped against an alley wall on a Father's Day morning. Foolishly reassuring him, "It's OK. Forget it. It's OK." Feeling his hand on my shoulder the night my mother died. The old aunt who raised him, walking two miles through a heavy snowstorm to get to the funeral home. The smell of her German kitchen, the rough but warm acceptance of his Italian relatives. The red and white of the Wildcats, the black and gold of the Braves. My folks dancing at his wedding. Getting roaring drunk the night before, grandly being shaved by a barber that morning, putting the ring carefully down on his palm and telling him for the hundredth time, "Don't drop the damn thing."

A thousand shared experiences...we still remembered.

He's a respectable insurance company executive in a glen-plaid suit now, the kid in the tight white T-shirt and the Levi jacket. And the silly maroon corduroy cowboy hat like the ones we wore hitchhiking through the small towns of central Pennsylvania one summer, hoping the rubes would say something smart and hoping they wouldn't.

This day, traveling on business, he wears a neat, red patterned tie.

"I remember when you couldn't have tied that damn thing for money."

"Yeah, and I remember when you thought a pink Mr. B shirt with a rolled collar and pegged pants were pretty hot stuff, too."

That was part of our bond, the easy insults we rained on each other, but wouldn't accept from anyone else. One night on the corner of 40th and Butler streets, a big Lawrenceville kid who had a girlfriend with wanderlust braced a few Garfield kids far from the safety of Penn Avenue and demanded: "Where's that sonofabitch, Musick?"

"Right here," snapped one of the strangers. In five minutes he had blood all over his face.

"I could've handled it," I protested later, stripping a couple of Band-Aids on his face.

"No, he was too strong, he would've kicked your butt all over the street."

I couldn't have listened to that from anyone but him and a week later, if memory serves, old Lawrenceville did exactly that.

Whole years seemed to pass when we were hardly ever out of one another's shadow. On the street. In dairy stores and pool halls, teaching the manufacturers of a hundred pinball machines the error of their designs with a small penknife or a long wire or, mostly, the pure skill we still recall with relish. On football fields.

Looking at him, I see the timeless smile; still cocky, but not quite as sure as it was then. A few people can grin with their eyes; he is one of them.

"Never got the nose job, huh?" I needle. It was badly busted in a sandlot football game when we were 16. We rushed a punt, I got the ball, he got a foot in the face. When they brought him down from the operating room later, the ether on him made me throw up.

No less mangled is the syntax he carried away from the Garfield streets. But I notice, as business finally puts an end to lunch, that acting in little theater and the feisty redheaded daughter of a well-to-do Germantown florist that he married 22 years ago have improved it immeasurably.

"Got to go."

"Yeah, me too."

We agreed that one day soon we'd get together.

"We'll raise some hell," he said.

Once we did. So we will again.

Another decade has passed and, God, in the single snap of a finger, we have been pitched deep into middle-age. Kids grown, careers on the downslope, bellies no more flat, time silently slipping away in chunks too huge to even contemplate, intimations of our mortality sitting there four-square in front of our eyes.

Living in different parts of the country, we are able to get together rarely. When we do, the years fade in an instant and we are back there on the streets of Garfield and Lawrenceville, where we came of age at one another's elbow. The bond between us is unbreakable, even by passing time and distance. All of those moments so central to existence—marriage, death, birth—we've shared. Best friends.

Can a newborn bring her mother into a new world?

KINDRA LEE WILLIAMS thrusts the tiniest of hands into the air over her bassinet and bawls lustily at the god of infants, perhaps protesting the circumstances of her birth. No one could blame her. She is a fetching baby, Kindra Lee is.

"Little girls be doll babies," her mother says. And so this one is—all fine, shiny hair and clean, bronze features and roaring indignation at being removed from the warmth of the womb. Lungs that would do an umpire proud. The nursery fairly trembles at her fury.

Down the hall in room 7504—the only one in the Mercy Hospital maternity ward with a sheriff's deputy at the door—Jo Ann Lowe sympathizes with the plight of her 2-day-old daughter.

"Life isn't easy," she says after a while, propped up in bed and looking as resilient as any freshly caught mother has a right to look.

"Life would be so much easier for you," a poet once observed, "if only you understood it is hard."

A lesson too late for the learning? Maybe. For the mother, anyway. Kindra Lee was damn near born in that great bastion of maternal instinct, the Allegheny County jail.

Bulging and under judicial fiat to reduce its population—"they always called me 'two people, or one and a half,'" Jo Ann Lowe laughs—the County Jail very nearly added another resident Sunday afternoon.

"They sometime feel the girls might be playing a game," Jo Ann Lowe explains, smiling at the silliness of anyone seeking comfort in a labor ward. "At the county, they want to see a show or your water to break. You ready, you walk down to the paddy wagon. I couldn't, so they had to get the ambulance. And they couldn't get one right away."

No complaint, that. Even behind bars, impending birth is celebrated. Kindra Lee will be claimed by any number of aunts and uncles. Matrons and prisoners fretted over her mother's diet; a soft mattress was located to ease an aching back. Some warmth percolated in a place that is largely cold.

"Those girls really took care of me," Jo Ann Lowe says. "I guess I was something special to them. They wanted me to have the baby over there."

The stereotype of the stern jail matron suffers at her hands.

"Oh, yeah," Jo Ann smiles. "They get you extra food. Bananas, pears...worry about your nutrition. A matron named Dober always carried a bag with things in it for me."

So, on a fine Sunday afternoon, did Kindra Lee Williams cause a breakout and first see the light of day at Mercy; new sister to David, 9, and Autumn, 4, who live with their grandma in Cleveland.

"My mother's coming Thursday to pick up the baby," Jo Ann Lowe tells a visitor very softly. Her eyes glisten. On Sunday, she'd been scared. She couldn't remember her mother's phone number. Somebody told her if she couldn't contact her, Kindra Lee might be institutionalized.

"It's hard," she says. "They told me my baby might have to go into a home. I was real nervous. But a social worker here straightened it all out."

For Kindra Lee.

For Jo Ann Lowe, the straightening out will take a while. She will go back to the County Jail, probably tomorrow, and be held there on a detainer filed by an Ohio law enforcement agency.

Maybe an Ohio judge will note Kindra Lee was born in a place named Mercy. Maybe he'll be a grandfather. Maybe he'll be a she. And maybe the next time Jo Ann Lowe sees her daughter, she'll be about ready for school.

Simply put, Jo Ann is a shoplifter.

Times are hard, she sighs, but she never went on welfare. "Economy the way it is, I was just trying to make ends meet..."

And the baby's father was out of work. And unemployment compensation ran out. And the stores stayed open late.

In her native Ohio, Jo Ann Lowe could draw a two-to-five-year prison sentence. A shoplifter; a drifter. David was born in Ohio, Autumn in Massachusetts, Kindra Lee here "because that's where her father is.

"That tells you I don't stay in one place very long."

Except jail.

The future...well, only a romantic would hold the notion that Kindra Lee's arrival is going to thrust her mother onto the paths of righteousness. Still, Jo Ann Lowe, well-spoken and gentle, hasn't exactly struck anyone as Dillinger. And babies have been known to bring about the turning of a leaf. And some stories do have happy endings.

"I don't know about a new leaf," Jo Ann Lowe says with a tired smile. "I do know I'm tired of going to jail. I'm going to stay out of those stores."

Try to, anyhow.

"Yeah," she says. "But it's hard to be legal, nowadays."

Hard to grow up with your Mom in the slammer, too.

Kindra Lee Williams is 11 now, as untraceable in the prison system-social services maze as is her mother. A caseworker tried to locate both the child and mother. "Nothing," she apologized.

Dozens of other pregnant women have been through the County jail since Jo Ann Lowe, who stood trial in Ohio. Maybe she eventually did "stay out of those stores."

Pretty to think so.

Will video craze faze Pinball Wiz's daughter again?

SOMETIME BEFORE SHE discovered boys and acquired mononucleosis—I strongly suspect a corollary there—my 14-year-old daughter lived a while at a video games arcade.

"Why,couldn't you just run away from home like a normal kid?" I finally asked her one night when her eyes seemed particularly glazed.

"It's a phase, Pops," she smiled. "It'll go away after awhile."

"You want to have children when you grow up?"

"Pops, they don't make you sterile."

Instinctively, I mistrusted video games. No need to tell the kids, but I was once known as the Pinball Wizard. Truth of it is, I could make them sit up and sing. Ballys, Williamses, the ones so old they didn't even have flippers, the ones that went tilt and confiscated your nickel when you breathed on them...wasn't a pinball machine ever made that I couldn't play Tchaikovsky on. And that's not bragging; that's confessing.

But who wants such a checkered youth for a daughter who is warm and bright and trusting. In short, vulnerable in a video arcade. A phase, she insisted.

So is malaria, I told her. I checked with similarly afflicted friends. "They're all doing it," I was reassured. I checked with the ophthalmologist. "Her eyes will eventually refocus," he promised. Finally, I checked the arcade over one night and had a short discussion with the guy running the place. "I smell anyone smoking a joint in here, I am going to close the cash register on your tongue." And then, grudgingly, I yielded to the craze.

Hell, I even tried to understand it. I tried Pac-Man. The cute, fuzzy monsters ate up my guy before he got his teeth into the first dot. I tried Space Invaders. I kept shooting up my own defenses. I tried pure logic.

"Those machines will give you zits," I warned.

They didn't. In time Pac-Man became a pale lure beside some tall kid with a mop of blond hair, and Keri Musick ultimately returned home from the video wars, wiser for the experience and deep into 1991's allowance.

"Told you, Pops," she said. "They were fun for a while, but they got boring. Too expensive. And..."

"Boys."

"That, too."

She's been off video games for months now and a lagging technology seemed about to spare future generations of parents the experience of asking a kid "everything OK?" and being told, "It's cool. Last night I got 7,695,420 on Centipede."

The operative word in the above sentence is "seemed." I take up your time with personal experience only to warn you that a new monster has recently been unleashed locally by Bob Schwartz, who otherwise seems a fine, young family man running an upstanding suburban business. So much for appearances. There is firm evidence that he has unleashed another video monster upon us.

It's an insidious invention called Gameline. Schwartz admitted guilt readily. Gameline, he explains, will carry the video disease to the penultimate. Where just weeks ago it seemed that tedium had videoitis on the run, a new species has raised its ugly head.

"The arcades were really tailing off," Schwartz explains. "A lot of them had already gone down the drain due to a lack of new, exciting disks. People got tired of shooting invaders out of space or gobbling up dots."

At the point of videoitis being arrested, the technology made a comeback and the other day Schwartz put Gameline into the local market. The details are complex to a guy who equates replacing a wall switch with brain surgery. Suffice it to say that for between $50 and $60, Bob Schwartz will sell you Gameline, which is packaged in the form of a fat cartridge. You plug it into the back of your home video game system—better you have mono in your house—and attach a wire from the cartridge to the back of a telephone.

Zap, you are plugged into a master computer which allows you to order up any one of about 100 new games and, depending upon your dexterity, play up to seven hours for a buck. The general idea is to let a customer try the games instead of shelling out maybe $30 for a bummer chosen from a catalog.

"How could you inflict this on the community?" I asked Schwartz, discovering that he is not altogether without conscience. Indeed, has known no few qualms about his business activities.

"I've thought about it," he says, admitting to being a bit squeamish over the number of video game cartridges sold to the unemployed. "But they say they've got to do something or they'll go crazy."

But to raise this craze from the dead?

"What's happening now is that video games are taking their rightful place as a diversion, instead of a compulsion," Schwartz defended.

Still unconvinced, I checked the patient.

"Look, kid, being bored with the mono and all, you're not going to start playing Ms. Pac-Man again, right? A phase, you said. Like purple fingernail polish and jeans that make your butt go numb, huh?"

"Don't worry, Pops," Keri Musick said. "Boys are more interesting."

Swell.

I am, as they say, having deja vu, all over again.

Some brief history. Keri Musick is now 25, running a restaurant, planning her wedding, talking about going to law school and in her dreams, sees tort reform and tortellini and tiaras. She hasn't been susceptible to electronic games since her junior prom. I have been blessed.

Conversely, I am once more cursed. Steven Marlier is 16 and in unashamed thrall to computer games, the viewing of which suggests the end of the world as we know it. He is a nice kid and I love his mother, which should explain why I am again confronted with this phenomena of little blue dots and other vulnerable sorts being eaten by indescribable creatures with huge mouths and various lethal appendages. In short, I am repeating a kind of parental experience that might easily explain child abuse.

Steve has tried to teach me to play these games. Better to have attempted to instruct the Venus de Milo in discuss-throwing. Still, I agree with my beloved daughter. It is a phase, not so different from the one I went through as The Pinball Wizard. To each generation, then, it's own form of mindless recreation.

Of Gameline, nothing is known. Possibly it was eaten by something.

Fishing fever catching in trek to rocky Maine coast

The middle-aged man and the sea...

As the swallows return to Capistrano and City Council to sheer foolishness, I yearly trek to the Maine coast; there to fish, idle, and inquire of the gods after an occupation which requires my presence so far from the ocean.

The sea's hold on me has long since been complete. Was it the night some years ago that I stood on a beach, watching a fierce storm 10 miles out light the entire sky off the South Carolina coast and saw shadowy shapes pitching and rolling in a desperate dash for the harbor? Or maybe the ocean won me with that very first lobster.

In any case, for a long time I've fancied that in some previous incarnation I went down to the sea in ships, or accompanied Ahab after the great white whale, or at least was around to snicker at the continuing rejection of Charlie the Tuna. Clearly, some deep, abiding tie exists.

Thus have more topical subjects been bypassed for this edition of the newspaper, sacrificed to the keen anticipation of killing some fish over the coming week.

This column, then, must necessarily be sort of a reverse of the what-I-did-on-my-vacation theme so popular with unimaginative schoolteachers. Your indulgence is mightily begged.

As you read this, I will have already taken rod-in-hand and begun serious thinning of the fish population of a quiet bay some distance to the South of the swells who, even this late in the season, clutter Bar Harbor with their huge Chris-Crafts. I will be the one in the doughty 14-foot aluminum yacht in faded jeans and heavy, weathered flannel shirt once bragged on by L.L. Bean.

For the next week, more serious and precise prose will occupy this rectangle and I'll wander the rock-bound coasts in diligent search of quiet; cheap lobster for the pot; and whatever fish might be lured by the ignorant. For the uninitiated...Mecca.

Although my saltwater fishing experiences are painfully limited and largely reduced to gawking at gulls and untangling backlashes, I am brim with confidence owing to a recent educational experience in the company of that renowned Cambodian angler, Phannak Srun.

A party of nine descended on the spillrace which drains Crooked Creek Lake in Armstrong County Saturday last in the conviction that (a) fishing promotes familial harmony; (b) man does not live by swimming, Frisbee and lunch alone; (c) some fine bass were there for the taking.

The sweet 16 in the crew excused herself early in the going to await the arrival of a young swain on a white charger; the lady allowed as though she might do a bit of sketching, and the rest of us fell upon the unsuspecting residents of the lake with something approaching blood-lust.

They won by knockout.

Familial honor, though, was rescued through the patient efforts of the second-youngest of the Sruns, Phannak—12 and distantly related to Izaak Walton —who yanked fair-sized perch from the water with a regularity which suggested his shoulders would grow two inches wider for the experience.

The person in charge, much better seasoned and given to lengthy instruction, suffered a shutout with abiding grace.

"One more, kid, and you walk home," Phannak Srun was told.

The day passed with no more than the usual number of squabbles, threats and parental dictums; the lady had some fine innings with a catfish larger of girth than Dave Parker, and the person in charge rededicated himself to the proposition that Mecca is, indeed, located catty-cornered to any body of water holding fish.

Back home, the head-of-household, nominally speaking, undertook a firm decision: A visit to a small town on the Maine coast was distinctly in order. There was to be, in no particular order of importance, a lot of fishing...only enough antiquing to prevent the lady from getting the bends...lobster enough to guarantee gout and sufficient spirits to prevent pinworms.

Tackle was sorted, rods readied, plane tickets purchased, and the imagination loosed like a moth around a flame-thrower.

Maine bay-fishing in Autumn is balm for the spirit comparable to Rip van Winkle's nap; guaranteed to return a man to the insatiable demands of a newspaper column almost cleansed of cliches and spoiling for further battle with the treacherous English language.

Form is everything, of course. Ideally, the fisher-person separates from all others a distance of no less than a half-mile. Lunch and white wine are packed along and the bottle buried to the cork at the surf line. Inquiries are made of the natives as to bait, locale, tackle and idiosyncrasies of the local fish.

A line is cast; tranquility arrives before the bait is wet.

Mecca.

> *I learned what I know of fishing—in truth, very little—along Fishing Creek in Clinton County. Which is where God vacations.*
>
> *As a kid, I pulled some cantankerous trout from the glittering sun spangles of that narrow, ever-rushing stream, but mostly I drowned worms and just sat there on a rock musing over forgotten pleasures and pains in the summer sunlight, and growing up.*
>
> *As a grownup, I fished a bit along the rocky Maine coast. Mostly, I caught Lobster Thermidor in nearby restaurants. What I like best about fishing is finding a remote spot where you can hear mosquitoes pass gnat gossip and think about not very much at all. Not what Izaak Walton had in mind, I suppose, but good for regenerating a flagging spirit or a weary body.*
>
> *My favorite fisherperson is the aforementioned Phannak Srun's older brother, Phanna (pronounced, incidentally, Puh-Naw). Once, wading to the knees in the spillrace mentioned earlier, he caught a 9-inch perch. Barehanded.*
>
> *It wasn't the first fish to succumb to his quick hands. In Cambodia, when the murderous Pol Pot was running things, Phanna did it often.*
>
> *"It's not hard," he still says.*
>
> *You might try it sometime.*

Pencils, Mysteries Share A Downtown Landmark's Cup

HE IS as familiar to the eye as a mother's smile. And in his way, as beguiling.

Maybe it's the sign, which has run through the imaginations of four generations of children hereabouts and proclaims both his blindness and his mystery. Or the face, richly black and as somber as stone. Or the old Philco, strung around his neck, a comfortable millstone blurting the message of whatever radio evangelist he's been able to dial up.

Or perhaps it is the sum of his other trappings. The dark eyepatch. The stark white visible in the uncovered eye, as though it had rolled way up in his head. The musette bag. The worn wool coat. The yellow pencils peeping from a cup hung on the radio.

Know him already, huh?

Know also that the Rev. Hosea M. Edwards—just months shy of his 80th birthday and by dint of long experience a serious practitioner of his trade—does not hold with panhandlers, streetwalkers, plain bums, cheats or solicitors of any sort.

"Nobody's making a chump out of me," the Reverend was grousing yesterday as the Downtown noontime crowds in front of Murphy's on Fifth Avenue swirled in front of his place of business. "Racketeers got two dozen guys like me on the streets, telling lies 'bout a man who's totally blind. For money!"

In fact, there could be no more than one Rev. Hosea M. Edwards than there could be a host of Taj Mahals or Ahabs or Abraham Lincolns.

For more than 35 years—rain or shine, the public avaricious or altruistic—he has sat just outside a door in front of Murphy's and sold pencils. Except Mondays.

Explains Angie, who can see the Reverend from her vantage point in Murphy's magazine department: "He don't work on Mondays."

The other four days of the business week, health permitting, he remains what he has been for almost four decades, a Downtown landmark of no mean distinction. "The one that has the radio? He's legitimate. Hell, he's an institution," says a cop.

To be bred hereabouts is to have often passed the Reverend's place of business and been briefly frozen in place by his sign: "I am blind. My eyes were shot out in the mines."

The Reverend has added a bit of romance there, the sign suggesting some human villain, rather than a random spark deep in a West Virginia coal mine that put an end to his eyesight at 27.

"Oct. 20, 1931!" he snaps, not unkindly but in the tone he brings to bear on anyone interrupting pencil commerce. "Logan County, West Virginia! I was putting two and a half sticks of black powder in a 6-foot hole with a tamping bar.

"It all went off in my face."

There was a school in West Virginia that taught the blind various trades, but it was segregated. He had left home in North Little Rock, Ark. at 16 with a fourth-grade education—roaming the country, farming and handling himself well enough to consider prizefighting as a trade—and there wasn't a whole lot to return to for a blind man. So, for the next 17 years, Hosea Edwards wandered the small towns of West Virginia, living on the streets and growing closer to the sort of Lord that Jonathan Edwards admired.

"I see people as saints and sinners," the Reverend explains. Martin Luther King was "wonderful"; Black Muslim leader Elijah Muhammad "deceiving."

The general public falls under a heading probably best described as "suspicious."

The Reverend gets flim-flammed by an occasional slug in his cup and he got a pretty good education from the mining company. Its insurance company settled $500 on him, but he felt the exchange hardly fair and filed suit. And lost. And lost his appeal. And, then, his innocence. His attorney turned out to work for the mining company. The discovery moved Hosea closer to God and farther from His creatures.

Long years ago, he became an associate pastor of the Nazareth Baptist Church in Washington, Pa., from which he buses to take up his station Downtown each morning at 9—"as soon as senior citizens can get on the bus"—and to which he returns early each evening, when the crowds thin and in their haste, grow chilly of heart.

His is a lawful enterprise, the Reverend would have you know, and he plans to pursue it "as long as the Lord lets me live." His health "tolerable," he expects that to be a while.

"My caseworker gets me a permit from the city every year to sell pencils," he says, a thunderclap from the radio startling a lady who has stopped to drop a few coins in the cup.

They add up to "'bout $10, maybe $15 on a good day," and supplement the $236 monthly Social Security check that supports him and his wife, Ruth, who's hospitalized. Clean money, he grumps.

"These others...well, people used to be scared to even come out on the streets and beg like that," he says indignantly. "My eyes...E-Y-E-S...were shot out. I'm totally blind."

Well, not totally.

"I can still see my God," he agrees.

That's all the Reverend deems necessary that he witness in this world, with a single exception:

"I would like to see my wife's face. I never have."

Hosea Edwards continues to uphold the tradition of what is still called in the rural South the "jack leg preacher." Itinerant pastors who spread the gospel wherever they find themselves and usually minister to several congregations.

The Rev. Edwards isn't on the circuit right now, but in July, he celebrated his 91st birthday and currently is a resident of a West Virginia nursing home. As soon as his ailing wife is again able to care for him, friends suspect he will return to the pulpit.

"His health isn't too bad," says the current minister of the Nazareth Baptist Church, the Rev. Charles Wyatt. "But he needs attention and his wife hasn't been able to provide it because she's ill.

"He's quite a guy. For years, before I switched fields, I worked Downtown and saw him a lot. Then, I came to take over this church, and there he was."

Yeah, Fifth Avenue between Smithfield and Wood hasn't seemed the quite the same without him.

Littlest Liver Patient Fights Huge Odds
Awaiting Transplant

The enemy is time, the race is with death, the hope is Dr. Thomas Starzl and...hard truth...the odds are rotten.

Still, in the two years little Janeen Fukahara has struggled for life, she has repeatedly survived such odds. Three major surgeries; three just slightly less so. Jaundice at birth, a liver functioning at three percent capacity, colostomies, a lethal blood disorder, rampaging infections, biweekly transfusions, a million needles, and endlessly chilling prognoses.

They had to rush Janeen to Children's Hospital Thursday night, not for the liver transplant she desperately needs, but simply to struggle with the disease which could take her life before you reach the end of this sentence. Yesterday morning, there she was, poking around in her crib, 104-degree fever and all.

She remains what she's been since May 3, 1981—pound-for-pound, as tough as rawhide. And as resilient.

If Janeen is the smallest liver transplant candidate in Children's Hospital annals, she remains the heavyweight champion of the field, a tiny 12-pound bundle of grit who couldn't sit up for more than a year. It would take five minutes to shake hands with all of the doctors who told her parents she would soon die. In a week, in a month, by Christmas.

"All the way, they kept telling us she would die," Susie Fukahara was saying yesterday afternoon, 2-month-old Cody riding her hip restively. "With the first surgery, they said she had a 30 percent chance to live. Otherwise, she would be gone in five months.

"Then, they told us there was a 10 percent chance if she had the second surgery and it worked. It didn't. They said 'she will die.' They kept telling us—three doctors, independently—'she's going, she's going...' It's pretty tough to take."

Clearly, the medical profession has underestimated Janeen Fukahara's determination and, perhaps, the curative powers of Christmas.

"The doctors back home all told us she would not make it to last Christmas," Susie Fukahara says. "That was the toughest of all. But we moved at Christmas and suddenly she started to gain weight and learned to sit up, and she made noises and gestures. She started to get better."

And Pat and Susie Fukahara started to fight the heavy odds lengthened by the towering fact that each day, 40 to 50 more kids need a new liver.

Doctors in Honolulu advised against a transplant: "One chance in a thousand." The Fukaharas saw Dr. Thomas Starzl of Children's Hospital interviewed on television and decided to take it.

Doors flew shut in their faces for months.

A liver transplant can cost as much as $238,000. They sued their medical insurance company after being told, "Sorry, your coverage doesn't include transplants."

They sought financial help all over Hawaii when their doctor told them, "Don't call until you have the money." They couldn't raise a dime.

They wrote to Children's Hospital here and received no reply.

They heard about the Minnesota Medical School, wrote, and got a crushing answer. A transplant was possible—if they could raise $100,000 in cold cash. "Up front," sighs Susie Fukahara in her lilting voice. "We...my husband is a construction engineer."

The insurance company stonewalled until a story about the lawsuit hit a local paper. "The next day we settled out of court."

"We started to bug Pittsburgh," Susie Fukahara laughs. "We must've bugged them enough."

Now, it is simply a race for Janeen's life. The Fukaharas have to relocate here so that Janeen is nearby if a donor organ can be found. Pat has to get a job, Susie has to find a place to live. Cody and Lori, 4, cared for. Money raised.

Some good people are helping: Sister Elaine Eckert, who runs Ursuline Center in Garfield and, ironically enough, is scrambling for money needed to complete a badly needed halfway house for just such families as the Fukaharas. The Greccos of Garfield, who have opened their home and are now part of one of the few Italian-Japanese households around. Judy Simmons of the Variety Club. Tony Cavaliere and Sister Suellen Brogan, caseworkers at Ursuline. The pros at Children's.

None, of course, can help with the biggest obstacle of all, time. In the last two years, it has run out on 71 kids at Children's waiting for liver donors. And even slight damage to a donor organ at removal, in transit or at implantation can cause a recipient to later bleed to death. And there is the chance of tissue rejection. And the liver is the most challenging of all organs to transplant. And Children's reportedly has only a 66 percent one-year survival rate after 139 attempts.

And still there is strong hope.

"We're here," Susie Fukahara says. "We'll wait and wait. It's all we can do now. I hope it's soon. We can't wait too long."

In fact, the wait was too long for little Janeen Fukahara.

The wait for a second transplant, anyway. Following a successful transplant not long after this was written, a second was required in the spring of 1985.

While awaiting it, Janeen contracted a serious case of the flu and her body temperature soared to beyond 103 degrees. Doctors at Children's had no choice when an appropriate liver became available.

During surgery on May 4, 1985, Janeen Fukahara, the smallest transplant patient in the hospital's history at that time, died. A ton of fight in a tiny body.

Memory flickers in close encounter.

I hadn't seen her in 28 years; hugging her didn't feel any different than it had when we were 17 and living that sort of sweetness that none of us ever knows more than once.

For a half-hour, I had sat in the noonday coolness of a quiet bar and waited for her as anxiously as I had the night I cautiously pinned a white carnation on her blood-red ball gown before the senior prom.

I was...what...scared? Afraid that reality would destroy in an instant a fantasy of her that I'd polished to a deep, rich luster across the decades.

Endless questions skittered through my thoughts. Had the neat tiny scar on her chin that I'd kissed affectionately—to silently remind her I considered it her only flaw—been erased by the decades? Would she, once nothing less than a wonderfully lithe professional model, have thickened some after six kids? Was there still enough of the devil in my 46-year-old eyes to make her blush and grin a little, because her essence would surely have remained that of the good Catholic girl she was?

Mostly, though, I wondered: Would she still remember some of how it had been between us at 17? Might just a little piece of that have survived the seasoning of life?

"You've filled out a little," I kidded, following her up the stairs to the dining room.

"Thanks a lot," she pouted and laughed over her shoulder.

I saw you last night and got that old feeling...

"What made you call me after all the years?" she asked.

It was complicated, I told her. Someone I'd known only for an hour triggered something in me that wanted to put aside ghosts. Or maybe I'd simply wanted to see how much of what she had been at 17—lovely, blonde, intelligent beyond her years, brimming with tenderness, as poised as a swan—had survived.

Of course, every last bit of it had, all but hair once the color of sunshine. Now it's a nifty shade of sand.

Mostly, though, I told her that I thought it was simply time.

"Only took me 10 years to get over you," I laughed. At myself.

We swapped life stories in 20 minutes. Her's orderly, mine disheveled. The whereabouts of old, lost friends. Where we had gone wrong individually in this world; where we hadn't. Sweet, sweet highs; some lows that lingered.

Places we'd been:

"Love San Francisco, hate New Orleans," she said.

"Your must not have seen the best of it."

"I did so."

"You couldn't have."

And, of course, unspoken but heartfelt: If you had seen it with me, Babe...

Reminiscences:

Our fathers, both dead. Her dad's favorite line: "Do you know the difference between a vision and a sight...when she goes to bed, she's a vision; when she gets up, she's a sight." Me telling her what I've always told people: It took me a long time to get over her; my old man never did make it.

Pictures of her kids and my sprawling crew.

"Glad they all took after their mom," I kidded her.

Like mine, hers are as lovely as spring. Faces flushed with her character and beauty, their father's wit and intelligence. One of them a flat-out show-stopper. Another whose picture froze my throat for a long moment, because I'd known her face so well for so many years.

Confessions:

"I never really believed in God until my first born daughter turned out to be a blonde with style and grace."

"My husband finally has been able to read your column the last few years."

Call me a hard loser: God, I loved that one.

We ate well, laughed a lot, choked up a couple of times, got caught up on the years, and both realized with a steady, steady look and not a word that what's between us now is history, and that long, gentle moment when what held us captive was each other.

And, of course, a tide of memories:

A silver charm bracelet holding the picture of a lanky kid she had lit up like Broadway. "Still have it in my jewelry case."

A night some street punks said the very worst thing they could have and, with a strength that surprised me, she'd insistently yanked me from harm's way.

Her mother.

"She liked you so much."

"I liked her a lot, too; she's quite a lady, but she was an enemy from there for a while."

"Why?" she asked, surprise in those blue eyes.

"We were kids but I wanted to grab you and run for the sun," I had to laugh. "She was too wise to let it happen. That's why I spent four years keeping you safe for college boys. But I finally forgave your mother. In 1974."

Her Aunt Mary, a marvel: "Didn't know she wrote me for a long time while I was in the service, did you?"

Our similarities: An abiding affection for animals, the joy of kids, a special place we didn't know we both like above most others.

Our differences: As always, her settled by some sort of inner peace; me still living largely on instinct.

A few hard times: Well beyond her now; for me, immediate.

In an hour, the ghost was long gone; the fantasy unmasked; a friendship buried by time, uncovered and painted with affection.

As there had been a time to meet, so was there a time to depart. It came easily, without awkwardness. There was another hug to leap 28 years in a blink. There was a final honest smile. There wasn't anything else. Maybe, some day, another lunch.

She dropped me off at the paper and ran her hand over my head, the way she must've done it with her kids a million times.

"Take good care of yourself."

"See you, Babe."

The fantasy had been terrific, I thought as her car pulled away. The reality was no less sweet.

In truth, I guess I loved her the way Bogart loved Bergman in "Casablanca." Never could quite put it away. Remember that great Bogie line when he was talking about he and Bergman and Paris: "Yeah, I remember...you wore blue and the Germans wore gray." Like that.

So, prodded by one of those cerebral itches that for me have always substituted for thoughtfulness, I called her and we had lunch. Back in the office, I wrote about it with the sense that many of you, too, had lived through a first love that had lingered out there on the horizon with the sunrises and sunsets.

Talk about Pandora's box.

Shortly thereafter, my marriage, badly teetering, went kerplunk.

"Everybody in Allegheny County knows how you feel!" What I did know was that sometimes the passage of time don't mean a thing.

Her husband took it with good grace but the eyebrows in their social circle got tangled in the hairlines. And nothing I had written before had savaged so many nerve endings.

Ten years to the month later, this past April, we had lunch again. Same restaurant. Hell, same table, I think. Same old feeling.

She still looked like Grace Kelley; I was still running helter-skelter though that maze I call my life.

There had been some changes. Her husband had died. I had made the acquaintance of yet another divorce attorney, and a long-term relationship had just ended.

As they say, no encumbrances. And, somewhere amidst looking back at what had been and ahead to what just might be, there was a long look you could've hung the wash on. The fateful scene in "Casablanca" would've paled by comparison.

You know something, after 38 years, I could still hear "I saw you last night and got that old feeling..."

Still can.

Bogie would've loved it.

Leukemia victim battles the odds with hope, patience

"CAN YOU DIE?" the kids finally asked one day.

She and her husband had talked about this moment for weeks. Feared it. Knew that it would arrive, as inevitably as the dawn. Should they wait until after the operation that would determine her future, and theirs? Or should she begin now to help them build their defenses?

"Yes," she took a measured breath and told them softly. The situation had to be clear now. She had gotten her own demons by the throat, she would help them subdue theirs.

"But everyone can die," she told them. "In a car accident, a plane crash. A lot of ways. With this, I could get better."

With the grit in Carol Kobus, you could repave the Parkway East.

Carol Kobus has acute leukemia. Two intensive five-day sessions of chemotherapy—the second of which very nearly killed her—brought about a remission. With a bone marrow transplant, she has a chance, half a chance, really, to see her three kids—9, 8 and 3—grow up.

"They say there's a 40 percent success rate; what they mean is you don't die," she says. Hope is now a number, 40.

Without the transplant, she could live three weeks or three years. No longer. The average is a year.

"That was the hardest part," she says. "Take the year with them, or risk the transplant and a chance of dying? A year seemed so short. Steven would be four, instead of three, that's all.

"I've tried to prepare them for whatever happens."

Don't misinterpret the words. The tone is stainless steel. Her vision is locked on the 40. You could find more self-pity in the writings of Job. This one is a fighter.

"When my hair fell out in the hospital from the chemo, I didn't even pay attention," she laughs. "I thought, 'How can you be vain in this?' When I got home, I took off my wig and the kids said, 'Wow! Just like a punk rocker!'"

Early in November, Carol Kobus developed a sore throat, which led to a routine blood test: "It showed leukemia."

Doctors told her that with intensive chemotherapy, there was a 70 percent chance of remission within five days. The chemotherapy didn't work. It was tried again.

"There were complications...a 106 degree fever they couldn't control," she says and laughs softly. "They didn't think I would make it. I fooled them."

The Carol Kobus Fund was formed by friends in the Bellevue area so that she will have a chance to keep fooling them.

On Saturday, Carol, her husband, Rege, and the kids will fly to California, where she will begin complex preparations for the bone marrow transplant at the UCLA Medical Center and cleave to that 40 percent hope.

"The operation itself is no big deal," she says.

The aftermath is a very big deal. The graft, from one of her five brothers, may not take. Infection is a major threat. And there is something called GVH (graft versus host) disease.

"It can be fatal," she says.

Medical insurance will pay only $70,000 of the expected $130,000 hospital bills, so some people are easing the way.

A fish fry and a PTA bake sale at the Bellevue YMCA raised $2,200. A representative from the Speedy Muffler Corp. called. Use its local franchise for a contribution drop-off point and the company would donate $5,000 to the fund. Two raffles are scheduled. The Steelers will play a basketball game against the Northgate High School faculty. A Monte Carlo night is planned. A golf outing. A teen dance.

"When I was in the hospital, a man mopping floors was really nice to me," Carol Kobus says. "One day, he asked me what it was like having leukemia. I told him, 'It's no 'Love Story', like the movie.

"But, you know, it really is. So many people have reached out to me. It's phenomenal."

The local parish even moved up 8-year-old Missy's First Communion so her mother could be there.

"She was a little afraid," Carol says. "She said, 'Don't leave me.'

"I said I'd stay right with her through the whole communion.

"She said, 'No, don't leave me; ever!'

"I said, 'As long as I can be with you, I will be with you.'"

I talked to Carol Kobus after the operation and she was still upbeat, still struggling against the odds, still looking down the road. But, she said then, the odds were long.

Too long. The next day, she ran out of fight. Or, more accurately, the leukemia prevailed. Before it did, in her quiet, gutsy way, she taught some people about the indomitability of the human spirit. And about the value of courage. And, maybe most of all, about dignity...in life... and death.

Boom Boom busts out of her shell, and what a shell

NOON IN A CROWDED suburban restaurant. She removes her coat and five people gasp. She's wearing a lavender belly-dancing costume. Her bosom, mindful of the prow of a rowboat, spills over her brief bra, a Niagara of flesh. Harem pants flutter about the thighs of a tackle. For belly dancing, she could not be better equipped.

She is about 5-5. She weighs about 250 pounds.

Their lunch forgotten, the patrons freeze as she moves among them to a booth along the far wall. You can feel the snickers, hear whispered disgust. All of that flesh...a healthy pink and freckled, maybe...but so much!

"Migawd, Harold, do you see that? Harold? Harold!"

She slips into the booth lightly, on a dancer's feet, and sips her coffee, those around her abuzz now, no longer staring but unable to stop craning. She pays them small attention.

Pat O'Hara quit hiding a long time ago.

And, as for Boom-Boom O'Hara, she collects the bug-eyed stares and whispers and giggles as though they were gold.

"It doesn't bother me any more," she says. "I enjoy it. Snapping their heads. It must be my deep need for attention."

Boom-Boom O'Hara gets plenty. For $60, you can buy her act. Belly-dancing. A voice with range and lilt. A cute, personalized poem. Good-natured humor. You want to defuse the office practical joker for a while; take the starch out of a cool, distant boss? Call Boom-Boom O'Hara.

"Boom-Boom's a fantasy person," Pat O'Hara says over her coffee. "I even call her 'she'. And, boy...she'll embarrass you. She'll light you up. She won't stop until the act is done."

Pat O'Hara became Boom-Boom two year ago as a favor for a friend who promotes oldie rock shows. The "Coasters" were in town. One of their standards had been a big hit years before, Little Egypt. Her friend wanted a Little Egypt in the flesh. Boom-Boom O'Hara was born.

"I came on, people went crazy," she laughs. "I tore the joint up. It was exciting."

So, working for both herself and a gag telegram company, she does eight to 10 gigs a week. In between, she cares for her husband and three kids, does the Lord's bidding, takes voice and acting lessons, and diets.

"I would never strip or do stags," she says. "The dancing only lasts a minute. I had to develop an act. All I want to do is be funny."

And maybe see her name in lights.

"Yeah," she says wistfully. "I want to be a star. On TV. A household name. Famous."

When Pat O'Hara used to look into the mirror, she saw a blob.

Remembered the night of the Verona High senior prom, when her date "played sick." Now, in her late 30's and at peace, she sees a vision of, oh, Ethel Merman.

"Growing up obese, it hurts so bad," she says. "You have to heal. But I found a way to live with the way I am. I learned to love myself. And I love my work."

No, Pat O'Hara doesn't hide any more. God, she is certain, don't make no junk.

"People in the church I used to attend said I was going to hell," she says. "I had friends there, I..."

Pat O'Hara doesn't go to that church any more, but she still tithes to a mission fund in India. And she doesn't hide.

Leaving the restaurant for a gig down the street, she hears more gasps. She strides purposefully to the exit, slowly pulling a coat over a bosom that would turn Dolly Parton chartreuse with envy.

"I'm in costume, I don't get concerned about the staring," she says. "It wouldn't be appropriate."

On this rainy day, the target is Bob Wissman, heir to the Wissman Bowling Supplies Co. on Ardmore Boulevard in Forest Hills. Outside the office door, Boom-Boom O'Hara slips off her coat and stands in the cold rain, fiddling with her tape recorder and waiting for an adrenaline rush.

"Nothing like show biz," she says, and marches in to the denouement of young Robert Wissman.

The hootchy-cootchy music comes up on cue and Boom Boom gyrates toward the victim: all bobbles, bangles, beads and 250 pounds of light-footed determination. Wissman takes root, then slowly begins to flee, backing away, blindly.

Everyone stands around, grinning like so many fools. Wissman runs out of room to retreat. Boom-Boom dances. Boom-Boom sings. Boom-Boom recites a glib, only slightly bawdy message. Boom-Boom does some quick stand-up repartee. Wissman blushes. The applause is spontaneous and warm. Boom-Boom exits gracefully.

"There is nothing like show business," she says, her costume threatening the traffic along Ardmore.

No, Pat O'Hara doesn't hide any more.

Not long after this was written, Boom-Boom's act went, well, bust. Retired, she is remembered.

"She was a good entertainer," says the woman who answers the telephone at the Eastern Onion Singing Telegram company.

And a rather gutsy lady. As the song reminds, it ain't easy being green. Pat O'Hara, a big person in more than one way, managed it with ease and style.

Baseball, medicine proved a demanding mix for Medich

HOLD THE TEARS and the laments for Doc Medich.

He could go to jail, but, if justice isn't just blindfolded, he won't. And he could lose a career for which he has struggled a full decade, but if common sense is brought to bear, that won't happen, either.

No, his history insists that what George Medich will do is to continue his treatment for drug dependency, stick his nose back against the grindstone upon which it has been so resolutely set since 1976, and someday down the road, get on with the repair of damaged human beings. That is his nature.

For a long time, Doc Medich danced on a very lean rope. Baseball demanded six months a year, medicine got six. He got what was left. He used to take such best-sellers as "The Journal of Bone Joint Surgery" on Pirate road trips and there were squint lines around his eyes when he was still a kid. He wanted baseball and he wanted medicine and he got both. Clearly, the price has been dear.

Doc Medich has always paid it. He played tight end on the Pitt football team and everything but water boy on the baseball team, and he was a schoolboy husband and father, and when he graduated from medical school in 1977, the dean said he was "an outstanding and remarkable student." And he was no less than either through an internship that used to keep him awake 36 straight hours twice a week. And he was, by all indicators, a fine orthopedic resident at a time when drugs got a grip on him.

Nope, sing no sad songs for Doc. He's been a stayer for a while. Kids shouldn't emulate athletes, but if they insist on it, Doc Medich would be a good role model. Still would, it says here.

As his Aliquippa mentor, Dr. Mickey Zernich, says, "George is a strong-willed person, practically minded. I don't think there is any doubt he'll be able to handle this."

"This" is presently a two-headed monster.

On Monday, Dr. George Medich was arrested on charges of improperly writing seven prescriptions for painkillers and muscle relaxants. The suspicion here is that 11 summers of throwing a baseball for a living might've had something to do with it, but that's conjecture. In any case, the damage wrought by those drugs, he bore alone.

Next month, he will face a hearing. That's dicey, but probation seems likely.

Sometime afterward, he will go before a more demanding tribunal of colleagues, who will determine his fitness for practicing medicine.

Both processes are delicate, so Doc Medich is keeping his own counsel for the time being, the whys and wherefores of his dependency unknown. Surely, unrelenting pressures had something to do with it, even if his wont as a ballplayer was to make light of them.

"Sure, there are some internal pressures," was a stock answer to people who wanted to know how the hell he managed to keep both baseball and medicine in the air at the same time, for so long.

Pitching at the major-league level is demanding, the act itself both an art and a science. Wrecked arms are not rare. Nor is chronic pain an unusual aftermath. Leaving the game behind can bring its own upheaval. As Jim Bouton once said, "You spend all those years gripping a baseball and then you discover it's been the other way around."

While Doc Medich plied his craft for six different clubs, medicine, the study or the practice of it, never got very far away, and presumably there was a toll.

"He's had a hell of a lot of stress in his life," Mickey Zernich says softly. "You know the stress professional athletes have, but almost all of them have a recovery period each year. When George was done with baseball, he'd go straight into a situation as stressful, or more so."

And handle it well. For three seasons, there were very few better baseball pitchers than Doc Medich and he probably never switched from flannel to civvies without a baseball writer asking, "Doc, how long you going to pitch?"

Medich pitched about as long as he could, until the last day of the 1982 season, and then immediately grabbed his stethoscope. It says something of him that the smoke apparently disappeared from his fastball before the Pirates signed him as would-be pennant insurance in 1976, but that he was still pitching six years later.

There's some sand in George Medich.

"He'll see the light quickly," says Zernich, "and recover from this."

You could make book on it.

Mickey Zernich was right, whatever Doc Medich's flaws, a lack of true grit was not among them.

Following a hearing on the drug charges, Medich was fined $5,000 and the Pennsylvania Board of Medical Education and Licensing placed him on two years' probation.

For more than a decade, he has practiced medicine in the Beaver Valley and currently has an office in Monaca. Controversy has continued to occasionally dog him. In 1989, a teenage boy died after Medich performed routine surgery on him to repair a broken shoulder. He was held blameless in the matter.

As Charles Barkley has noted, athletes do not necessarily make ideal role models. Doc Medich did, and does.

Victim of fatal beating anything but a park fixture

HE WASN'T A BUM or a vagrant or a dummy, or a threat to anyone or anything...and those who put him in the ground this morning would not like him remembered that way.

Misfortune simply got a grip on Ralph Novak before he was a year old and didn't let go until just before noon today, when he was mourned throughout St. Augustine's parish in Lawrenceville and prayed for in the mass of Christian burial.

The family had asked the coffin be left open during the viewing. The undertaker finally agreed, but he took Joe Domyslawski aside and told him, "Don't let any of the women kiss him, or touch his face at all...it's that bad."

Early Sunday morning, the cops say, two teenage kids shook Ralph Novak from a deep sleep and then beat him to death for no discernible reason. An ill-fated prank, it's been suggested.

Ralph Novak might've expected it.

When he was nine months old, a little cousin accidentally jabbed his eye out with a pencil. When he was 10, he was involved in an automobile accident in Sharpsburg that left him unconscious for a week. When he was 32, he was hit by a car and suffered irreversible brain damage.

Thirteen years later, to the day, he was slain while he was sleeping on a bench in Arsenal Park.

"His body was dragged all over the park...like he was a bag of garbage," says Joe Domyslawski, whose wife, Florence, was Ralph Novak's sister.

"From a kid on up, he had nothing but hard luck that I could ever see. We don't hold any malice, my wife and I, but my brothers-in-law got anger. You can see it in their eyes."

Some of the anger in the Domyslawskis and the Novaks comes from the senseless killing of a harmless man, some from the fear that people are not quite clear about how Ralph Novak was.

He was "a little slow, maybe," as they say in the ethnic neighborhoods.

"He would do something one day, he might not remember it the next," Joe Domyslawski says. "But he would three days later. He wasn't stupid or any-thing."

With the slowness, there was also a kind of innocence.

"You wouldn't believe the way kids took to him," Domyslawski says, not noticing the irony in the words.

Ralph Novak worked, and he doted on children, and no one ever asked him for help twice. And if he had to die the way he did, his people say, then the record ought to be clear.

"The TV said he was a permanent fixture...was he a park bench, screwed into the concrete? A tree with roots in the ground?" Joe Domyslawski asks. "I want to tell everything about him."

So, for the next half-hour or so, Domyslawski does. He talks about Ralph Novak caring for some of his 10 brothers and sisters. Drawing a little Social Security insurance check. "Always working to make a few dollars. He wasn't any bum."

No, Ralph Novak was not a bum. He was, in fact, a damn good painter. Had just finished a sister's house in Crafton the day before he was killed. He loaded and unloaded trucks in the Strip. Did odd jobs. "And he helped anyone who ever needed it."

And often he sat in the park. Mostly, he took nieces and nephews there to swing. Occasionally, he'd have a couple of beers and fall asleep in the sun.

"One beer, with the brain injury, made him woozy," Joe Domyslawski explains. But understand, his brother-in-law was no vagrant, no mindless body huddled on some bench.

"They said he was a permanent fixture in the park," Domyslawski says, anger creeping into his voice. "He didn't just wander around. He was always going someplace."

To whatever job he could find. To a little place on Butler Street where he made an occasional football bet. To shoot a little pool and drink a couple of beers. To the home of a brother suffering from cancer. To the hospital to see a sister with multiple sclerosis.

For years, he had wheeled her a couple of miles every day, along Butler Street and up a steep hill to see their mother. He and his sisters had always had a special closeness.

When they were kids, one of them, Patricia, wrote a letter to a newspaper that attracted attention: "Santa, I don't want any toys or anything...just give my brother a new eye."

"He was a good-looking kid, but when he talked to you, he'd always turn his head away," Joe Domyslawski says. "On the bus, people would stare at him, and he would cry or swear at them."

"Anna wrote that letter and Ralph got a new eye," a transplant arranged by a Good Samaritan.

And then he got hit by a car and had seizures for two years, and after that, Ralph Novak lived in his own place and time.

"He was a...free soul," Domyslawski says. "Oh, he met girls, but it never turned out. He'd get jobs, but he never held them long."

In time, along Butler and up the narrow, numbered streets past Penn clear to Liberty, whenever someone needed help—move furniture, paint a home—they would call Ralph Novak.

"Everyone knew him, go ask around," Joe Domyslawski says softly, "and he never refused anybody anything. And he never hurt anybody."

Now, nobody can hurt Ralph Novak.

You could look at it this way: the senseless killing of Ralph Novak was maybe our first unmistakable signal about how cheap life around here has become. Novak's death shocked people 11 years ago; today it would not.

The Domyslawskis and the Novaks think Ralph Novak's killers got off cheap. After separate trials, in which they were tried for second-degree murder, Joseph McManus got a 10-to-20 year sentence, Mark Michalski received 8-to-10 years.

As Michalski was about to be taken from the courtroom, one of Novak's relatives shouted, "Go on! Lock those cuffs on him."

Joe Domyslawski is retired now and suffers from arthritis in both hips. He remains bitter about Novak's death.

"Those two boys are out now, I think," he says. "The trial was a farce as far as I'm concerned. One of their uncles was a cop. So..."

Life Flickers On The High Wire
But A Pro Cheats Death

HE WAS A pro, he reminded himself when his feet screamed at him that it was suddenly going wrong. That it could kill him.

Still, no one had ever done it. Not the Great Wallenda, not any other wire-man, had ever walked one-half mile across the Mississippi River. He kept going.

The steel cable, a bit thicker than his thumb, began doing a slow rhumba when he was a hundred feet out from the eastern bank and 265 feet above the water.

It's OK, I can handle it!

To fall was simply to die. It always is.

He was afraid. He always is.

The river was rushing to the sea at 17 mph. Below, a tug strained to hold a barge steady. Maybe 100,000 people—drawn to last May's kickoff celebration for the 1984 New Orleans World's Fair—crowded the banks. Like all those who have ever looked up at him, something inside them hoped to see him fall.

"I hit the river from that height, I'm dead," he says off-handedly. "Survive the fall, I'm food for the sharks in the Gulf of Mexico."

The engineers had screwed up and now the cable began cracking like a whip in an angry man's hand. He walked on, feet as sensitive as fingertips clutching the cable.

I can handle it!

The wind blew up hard against his back and the cable began undulating like heavy surf. The wash from a television station's helicopter, suddenly 30 feet off his shoulder, owned the cable. Winking seductively in the afternoon sunlight, the Mississippi suddenly yawned at him.

Jay Cochrane couldn't handle it.

"Now, I'm running on the cable with my feet sideways. It's doing 360-degree turns, two or three at a time. I'm grabbing at it with my toes and it's spinning off my heels."

One of the great skywalks ever was over.

"A stunt," he says, briefly feeling the freak. "Another Evel Knievel!" he mocks.

Like Knievel, Cochrane survived. For a lifetime, 38 minutes, he clung to the cable while it was lowered, suffered no worse than a nasty gash in his thigh, and for the next three weeks, you'll be able to look up at Kennywood, 24 hours a day, and see Jay Cochrane. Living on the high wire, 100 feet up.

"I almost lost my life, almost blew a 27-year career," he was saying at the park in the morning, sipping orange juice in a deserted restaurant.

Almost only counts in horseshoes and hand grenades. Walk the high wire for a living, almost occurs a lot - at 4:30 and 9:30 p.m. daily. It's what makes ice form in the spectators' tummies.

"The little ones keep you going," Cochrane says, shrugging. "The big ones get you notoriety."

Kennywood is a little one. He'll sit up there on a couple of boards 24 inches wide for three weeks. Walk the wire 500 feet twice every day but Mondays. Suffer the elements. And maybe, when he gets tired and bored, look down and remember his hometown, Toronto, 1965, and the day he fell.

Like New Orleans, he had left the responsibility for stringing his rigging to others. A tower collapsed and he dropped 40 feet like a shot. "Broke both legs...both arms...both feet...my pelvis...four ribs...and my collarbone."

But not his funny bone.

"Yeah, I learned something from Toronto," he says, "don't let anyone else touch your equipment."

A doctor told him he would not walk again; Cochrane was four years healing. He spent it acquiring a master's degree in structural and bridge engineering. Then he went back to the wire.

"It's what I do," he says.

And has been doing for 27 of his 42 years, a kid who, well, "ran off and joined the circus." For a while, he was the one walking behind the animals with the shovel. Now, at 42—blond, crisp but friendly, and so tautly-muscled he could not be pinched with pliers—he does six different aerial acts.

He lived for three weeks on the wire in Puerto Rico—six shows daily, 17 miles in three weeks—and then completed the walk between high-rise buildings that killed the great Karl Wallenda.

"I wanted to live on a wire higher than he walked on."

Always, it's higher, farther. Cochrane seeks financial support to walk three-quarters of a mile across the Chicago skyline, 1,470 feet up. No one's ever done it higher, farther. "The longest aerial walk ever done," he enthuses.

He wants to walk across Niagara Falls. It was done once, decades ago, the most famous wire-walk of them all. He wants to duplicate it; says he has been fighting the Falls commission for five years for permission.

In April, he's going back and walk that 2,640 feet across the Mississippi. Beat back the fear. "If you're not afraid, you don't belong up there."

Does anyone? Sure. Because the Mississippi is there, just another Matterhorn. And because "nobody's ever done it." And because, "Hey, I'm a professional."

Jay Cochrane's eyes glitter at that. Amusement? The cliche every wireman hears endlessly—a death wish?

"Professionals don't make mistakes, do they?" he smiles.

Some do...once.

A decade or so later, he still hasn't made that walk above Niagara Falls or across the Chicago skyline, but at 52, he's still up there on the high wire. Still doing the little ones that keep him going and the occasional big one that gets his name in the papers or his feet on the tube.

"Yeah, still at it after all these years," he says. Occasionally, Jay Cochrane returns to Kennywood. Spent a lot of August working in Pennsylvania...making them look up and feel the little tickle of ice in their stomachs. Wherever he works, the result is always the same. Throats get a bit tighter, eyes strain to pick him out against the sky or in the floodlights. Lots of gasps before he finally reaches the other side.

Cochrane, doing some booking on the side these days, doesn't know when he'll retire. He continues to hope the choice is his.

City Priest Offers A Safety Net For
Steel's Social Fallout

SOMETHING DON'T break for me soon, my best bet's the bridge," he was telling a social worker last week.

He is 52. An unemployed city steelworker, dumped just weeks away from earning a pension by the company with the conscience of a grape. You could hide a snake in the valleys that line his face.

When he was beered up, he used to like to say that he'd "starve before he took a dime from anybody". The gut boast of the millworker: Independence is always right there at the end of your arms. Now, he gets groceries from a food bank; goes late, when no one's around. The $50 a month or so he saves goes in a saloon on Butler Street.

He and his wife don't talk much. He had all the answers she needed for 30 years; now he doesn't have any. It dries up conversation. He used to raise his kids with laughter and the back of his hand; now it's all hand and they wonder if he gives a damn. Sometimes he doesn't.

He used to swagger on the streets like a shore-leave sailor. Now, he stays home. His name doesn't matter; when autumn came to the steel business here, it left a neighborhood full of him.

Every once in a while, he tells someone he might kill himself.

He's one of Father Rich Zelik's people.

For six years, working out of a cluttered office in the basement of St. Augustine Church on 37th Street, 10 strides up the cobblestones from Butler, Rich Zelik has been juggling the social fallout from steel's death dance.

Anger; the chilling apathy that replaces it. Drugs, depression and despair. Wife-beating. Torn pride. Child abuse. Self-loathing. The good stuff.

For six years, he read everything he could find about the steel business; braced industry executives at public meetings; and told everyone in Lawrenceville that hard times weren't more than a few paychecks away.

"I have to be objective," he was saying cautiously yesterday morning, thoughtful silences punctuating sentences. There is some anger in him; he hides it well.

The steel executives who have lied to him wouldn't fit in his church. One got up at a public meeting a while back and assured a group of Lawrenceville workers that his company had no plans to shut down.

"It was gone in a year," Zelik says. "I have a brother who had done serious research into emerging patterns in the steel industry. I knew changes were coming. I realized they were here when I read that companies were bringing in headhunters to trim personnel."

The headhunters have come and gone. So has a lot of Lawrenceville's lifeblood—the steel-related employers. Nobody bothered to look back.

"There has been a lack of respect for what the workers have done," Zelik says softly, which is the way he says most things. "Big steel created this community...you don't just walk away."

From places like Lawrenceville, the steel giants ran.

For years, a lot of empty three-piece suits got up in halls on Butler Street and in the Mon Valley and talked about the coming resurgence. Hang tight, they told out-of-work steelworkers, a brave new world was coming. They lied in their teeth.

"That's what big steel is doing, stringing people along, not telling them that it's not coming back," says Zelik. "They justify it by saying they can't reveal strategic corporate planning."

They had a willing audience. On Butler Street, there are still believers. So-and-so was called back, they tell one another on the street. So-and-so is retiring. Jobs will open up. Like hell. Big steel loves sheep.

"On the floor of a mill," Zelik says, "the men were trained to walk away from decisions. That was left to someone up the line.

"What are they supposed to do now, change overnight?"

Know this. Rich Zelik is not some latter-day Wobblie, stirring a workers' revolt; not some street demagogue unwilling to acknowledge a sputtering industry's problems. He is a quiet, bald, overworked, 40ish Capuchin parish priest left to grapple with the legacy of unconscionable big business.

"These are good people around here," he says, "and they don't know where to turn."

Some do. To booze.

"A big problem, getting bigger," he says. "And drugs among the young kids, the 19- and 20-year-olds who can't find work. I hear it. Something happens, the kids say, 'Well, he was high.'

"There's a lot of stress in the homes. Violence. Depression."

Some turn to the church.

"I tell them, 'You bring your world in here, God touches your life out there'," he says.

God or that other would-be savior, high tech.

"We're talking men in their 40s and 50s, who can't be retrained," Zelik sighs. "That scares them. To save their dignity, some take jobs that pay half what they used to make. Some lose their anger and don't care. Then, what's that teach the younger people? That the giants in their life are out of control."

Which happens when they're out of work.

"What we're trying to do," Rich Zelik says, "is tell them that if you're out of work, you are still somebody."

The locale has changed, but Father Rich Zelik is working the same old gig. This time it's in Charleston, West Virginia, where the chemical industry there is about the same place steel was around here a decade ago.

His business now, as it was then, is helping pick up the pieces when an industry decides the bottom line obliterates its responsibilities to the people who built it.

"Same kind of blue-collar area, racially-mixed," Rich Zelik says with a small smile in his voice."I've been here before, you might say."

He left Pittsburgh a couple of years ago after transferring from his St. Augustine parish duties to the field of social justice, in which he worked for nine years. Helped start the Tri-State Conference on Steel. Worked for the Franciscans at the United Nations. Moved on to Charleston to oversee St. Anthony's and experience deja vu.

"Education for the children became a struggle," he says of his St. Augustine days. "What happened to steel created tension in the homes. A lot of dreams were lost. That parish, people-wise, didn't bounce back."

Great Corned Beef Has Followed The King Into Extinction

THE KING of Corned Beef would sit on a folding chair in front of his little grocery store on Mellon Street and rub his bare feet.

In time, he would grudgingly accept the presence of a customer, fixing him with the baleful, threatening look of a Doberman.

Behind black eyes hidden beneath hedgerow eyebrows, a decision would brew slowly. In ways understood only to him, customers were either worthy of his efforts, or they were not. Usually the latter. Goyim could occasionally be seen quaking under his gaze.

He was older than God; his bent back reminiscent of a horseshoe. Unexplained anger and fatigue always seemed at war for him.

And the sensitive trembled in the presence of his genius.

His corned beef was leaner than a shadow. Even of texture, just an oblique suggestion of the brine which made it what it was, an unspeakable delicacy. Fringed with the precise amount of fat which separates the genuine from the poseur. Fresh to the mouth, it did at first blush what all great corned beef must —curl the tongue in sour surprise and bring forth from the salivary glands a flood tide.

Kosher dills were invented for the sole purpose of simply doing no more in life than lying there on the plate in humble accompaniment of the old man's marvel. Cold beer, likewise, knew no greater purpose.

It was said that the rubbing of the old man's feet was what gave his hand-wrapped corned beef its character and distinction.

Bearded by the customers he suffered unwillingly, he would at long last either heave from the chair, or growl in explanation points: "Closed! Closed now! Come back tomorrow!" And then his lined face and empty eyes would leave the impression that the earth had just yawned and swallowed the uninvited.

But even those slinking away, did so planning their return at some more opportune moment, perhaps in an hour when the desperation of their need was a match for his grouch.

He was truly the King of Corned Beef.

Some 25 years ago, the gnarled old man died and the earth wrenched mightily as he carried his secrets to the grave. His mourners were legend, in numbers and grief.

Given no choice, they passed his mantle on to one Jerry Fox, an outlander from Squirrel Hill and a lesser genius, to be sure, but ultimately worthy. Alas, Fox is currently cooking in a Downtown fast-food joint in which no self-respecting brisket would be caught dead and the brutal truth of the matter is now flush upon us.

This city—with its share of Jews, with its skyline changing almost hourly, with its rich ethnic mix—is flat bereft of decent corned beef. To say nothing of respectable chopped liver, pastrami, dills that screw your tongue into a granny knot, and any sort of decent cheesecake unadorned with the fruit that only savages put on it.

About here, it seems prudent to establish my unyielding credentials in this matter. It is quite possible that I am the world's leading gentile authority on Kosher food: Having grown from puberty into deep adolescence in the kitchen of a lady named Klein; having worshipped at the wondrous feet of the King of Corned Beef; and being the only man of Scotch-Irish descent you probably know who can whip up a blintz in the time it takes to sneeze.

I offer as further credibility the testimony of sportswriter Bob Smizik, with whom I once had the following conversation.

Me: "Listen, I know more about Kosher food than you do."

Him: "That's preposterous, I'm Jewish."

Me: "Nevertheless."

Him: "Prove it. Where do you get the best corned beef in town?"

Me: "From an old man on Mellon Street in East Liberty, when he's in the mood."

Him: "Can I have your recipe for chopped liver?"

Corned beef and related subjects rest heavy on the mind these days with word of the passing of the sainted S&B, fallen from culinary grace on April 24 last owing to problems having to do with landlords and bankers and exterminators.

"It was an institution," former owner Jerry Fox was saying the other day. "It was a heartbreaker to give it up."

For 49 years, the S&B Sandwich Shop peeked out on Oakland from a niche on the Boulevard of the Allies, next to whatever car dealership was occupying the building next door that week.

It was all sound and fury, the accouterments heaped upon one another and in constant danger of falling and crushing the wedge of people who crowded it from sunup to midnight.

Pearl Walker bustled ceaselessly, demanding in full throat, "Salami, eggs over, rye toast, coffee!" Plates were tossed at you, service the victim of unpretentiousness. Split-shift guys bought Iron City by the bottle, arguing the critical issues of the day—the Steelers and sex. Old Charlie shuffled through his busboy chores as though walking on live coals. The sizzling griddle threw the smell of good, clean grease into the air clear to the huge refrigerator in the corner, which held the beer, ate up half the tiny place and dominated it like a 500-pound canary in a parakeet's cage.

It was possible, nay likely, to find Steeler tackle Larry Brown delicately destroying the sandwich named after him—corned beef, egg, melted Swiss, lettuce and tomato. Or Fox staring holes in the raucous kids from the Job Corps on Forbes. Or maybe debonair Robert Wagner, the actor over from the

Playhouse, jammed at the counter between the Joyces, who stopped by every night for beer (him) and corned beef (her) and came around the day the S&B closed for good. Or Fritzie Zivic carefully working a sandwich under his battered, meandering nose.

On April 24, that day of infamy, Jerry Fox had to lock up for the last time. Marked was the passing of great local corned beef from endangered species to extinction.

The King of Corned Beef is dead. Long live the King of Corned Beef.

On that revered site, where the King of Corned Beef once worked his magic, sits...damn...a superette. And this town remains bereft of decent corned beef. And do not tell me anyplace with "Bubble's" in its name is capable of producing worthwhile corned beef. The S&B was its last refuge.

Oh, I know, there are delis in Squirrel Hill, and even Shadyside, perish the thought, which lay claim to selling excellent corned beef. Impostors, I assure you.

Is there not a true Jew, anywhere in this place, willing to make the sacrifices necessary to doing justice to a brisket? No, now we have delicatessens bragging about that bastardized version...the Reuben. A silly sandwich, if ever there was one. Melted, gooey Swiss cheese on corned beef? Thousand Island salad dressing, for God's sake? Better to marry chocolate syrup and asparagus!

In retirement, I, an Irisher but with passionate devotion, plan to take up the cause. Not that I'll ever become the King of Corned Beef. Ah, but the Prince of Pastrami, perhaps.

When Life's Unforgettable Lessons
Were Learned On Cue

THE PLACE STAYS in my mind, like a first kiss. Or a first bloody nose or visit from the first bill collector.

The sweet heft of a nicely balanced cue. Keeping a Pall Mall in the corner of your mouth when you shot, so that the halls of smoke would drift up into the lights instead of your sinuses. Clouds of talc floating down on fading, green felt. Warm beer going stale. Sweat born of staring too long at the eight ball.

Nothing smells quite like a poolroom—the sour union of a gym, an ashtray and a urinal.

Still, the memories linger somewhere there under my sternum, truth to tell, walled off with the other relics of youth. Called up only in occasional longing and surprise at how quickly middle age can fall upon you.

Poolrooms served as incubators for the generations who never knew Sesame Street. But did know the character-building traits of call-shot. Who came of age, not in front of a television set, but leaning on a cracked glass counter-top held together with duct tape and the faith of a thousand elbows.

Some of what's wrong with the world these days, I'm certain, can be traced to the lack of poolrooms. To boys growing up without the rough and raucous aging to be gotten in them.

I made that discovery the other day waiting for a bus in front of a building which, when I was growing to uncertain manhood back in the Paleolithic Age, was a poolroom. Dank, dirty, dim, delightful. Bogie in Casablanca never held any more intrigue.

I hope they bury me standing up in the corner of such a smoky place; one with a sign on the wall that says: Spitting permitted, scratch on the eight ball is a loser, no broads.

For 45 years, man and boy, I have been a lover of poolrooms. Their mystery. "Guy's got a two-piece cue!" Their excitement. "A fin? Hey, 50 or nothin', sucker!" Expletives torn from utter anguish. "Sonofa...I ought to stab myself with this damn thing."

I have written of poolrooms; once returned to them with the faith of a swallow to Capistrano; paid homage to them in defiance of Thomas Wolfe. And finally, abandoned them when they came to have kittenish names like Cue 'n Cushion, and orange felt, and, by God, women. There, sadly, I was forced to draw the line and reserve for them naught but bittersweet reflection.

Boys grew to maturity in poolrooms. In one, I learned that sex wouldn't necessarily make you blind, although it was always suggested that warts were a distinct possibility. In another, I came to understand that there is good in evil people and evil in good people, and that sometimes it's hard to tell the difference, but if you can, it will make your pockets jingle.

Pittsburgh Places — Pittsburgh People

I've grown away from poolrooms, of course, what with my involvement with kids and crabgrass and golf—a dull, clumsy kind of rotation pool. In truth, my cue never quite made the transition from the mean streets of Garfield to the tepid ones of suburbia.

My kids, sad to say, have never been in one. It is their loss, poolrooms being the places where boys of forgotten summers first came to grips with life's realities. Discipline, poverty, failure, loyalty, triumph, risk. Encompassing awe.

It was in a poolroom that I once shook the pudgy but legendary hand of Rudolf Wanderone. Fat Man, I desperately wanted to assure him, I too, have risked it all on the nine ball. I, too, have had wavering concentration allow some unflinching stranger access to my pocketbook. In fact, at that moment of moments, I almost swooned in the very presence of, and was dumbstruck by, Minnesota Fats.

Serious discipline, in my neighborhood, was taught less by parents and more by Red, the hard, silent guy who ran the poolroom on Penn Avenue. Once, he threw a beer salesman into the side of a fast-moving 88 Frankstown streetcar and then kept us ruly with only frosty, blue eyes.

The lesson of loyalty, I probably owe to Johnny, now doing life because one evening a guy he was arguing with over a girl suddenly died, owing to his head hitting a steam radiator. Before that, Johnny was the poolroom protector of our slender rights, so when he went up for murder one, we sent him cartons of Chesterfields to the prison; speak kindly of him to this day.

Poverty was first stumbled over in the process of not owning a quarter for the slop eight ball games, and, more, by the poolroom rummy, who swept the cigarette butts out on to the sidewalk every morning for a nightly flop on the bench in the back.

Kids today learn such lessons in different, and I suspect, less indelible ways. Could Misterogers ever fill them so full of confidence as taking away the lunch-money of a kid named Spike? He dressed—Preppie, the kids would call it now—and thought looking like a racetrack tout was all there was to hustling pool. Glory be to whatever, I spent my teens painstakingly disabusing him of that notion.

Such an environment nudged us slowly on to our majority. In the poolroom, we first transported with men; carefully, but at times equally, on the steadiness of our eyes and youthful nervous systems. There, under their restraints, we sneaked that first beer, forbidden and sweeter than any ever would be, again.

Time passed, the lessons were gleaned, and I lost my touch. Can't shoot worth a lick anymore. The poolroom has been an appliance store for years.

But Wolfe was wrong.

I have shot eight-ball, French, nine ball, straight, whatever, in more places than I can remember. In a number of churches, occasionally beseeching God for good table position. In shadowy joints where dirt eddied in every corner and cops often peered through the gray-streaked windows. In rooms brightly-lighted where, sadly, could be heard the squeal of women. In suburban basements with cues someone had sat on, where ease never comes. And, once, on a table with no pockets in a rich man's house.

I have won money, and lost. Played, often, with nothing at stake save pride and the pure sense of accomplishment that comes when the final ball nestles into a pocket and you get to say, casually, "rack 'em."

The Music Man be damned.

After a decade hiatus, I have taken up the cue once more.

Still can't shoot worth a lick, really. But, every once in a while, muscle-memory kicks in and a delicate touch returns from very far away, and I will gently cut a ball into a side pocket from an impossible angle. The ball will float...float...and settle into the pocket as a returning dove does to its nest. And, momentarily, I will again be 17.